T
PROI   SON

MW00895830

From Dope Dealer
to
Hope Dealer

REVISED EDITION

An Autobiography

By
V. Ricardo Thomas, Sr.

Prodigal Son Ministries
16548 Hamilton Avenue
Highland Park, Michigan 48203

www.prodigalsonministries.org
Prodigalson9988@aol.com

FOREWORD

Pastor Rick is a passionate minister with a fiery message for the youth of today, their families and church community. It's rare to read a book that taps every emotion; this one does. I laughed out loud, I wept sorely; I prayed over the many people whose lives were impacted. You will relate to the various "folk" mentioned in his book as though they were your own family and friends. God hears the cries of your heart. Those whom you love dearly have not done too much or strayed too far. God can bring back a prodigal from the ends of the Earth. Pastor Rick's testimony is a witness to what God can do in the lives of those who are prone to wander even when they have been rooted and grounded in the Word.

Sabrina D. Black*, MA, LLPC, International Speaker, Counselor and Author of: "Can Two Walk Together?" "Prone To Wander" "HELP! for Your Leadership" and "Counseling in the African American Community;" President, National Biblical Counselors Association; Chairperson, Black African American Christian Counselors.*

The amazing story of V. Ricardo Thomas is truly a modern day depiction of the parable of the Prodigal Son. His gutsy story telling style takes you with him on a blood curdling journey from being a young person brought up in the church to a highly committed, career criminal and back to the church, by God's mercy and grace. Through all of the madness recorded on these pages God's hand of care and compassion are magnificently portrayed. Reading this great book will give you hope for the prodigal in your own life.

Joseph Williams *– Author – "Sheep In Wolves' Clothing...When the Actions of a Christian Turn Criminal" Executive Director – National Association Prison Aftercare*

*As an author of several books and reader of many, some books get my attention and others I can't wait to get done or simply just put down. Speaking from the mind of a former brother from the streets of South Philadelphia's hood, my schedule today (as a husband, father, pastor, president of several ministries, conference speaker, on several boards, seminary student and life) doesn't allow me to pick up a lot of other things; which includes reading boring books that are going no where at all. However, when it came to this book, I saw my life unfold right before my eyes. It was as if, Ricardo was telling my story for me but it was his own. "The Prodigal Son" got so much of my undivided attention that **I COULD NOT PUT IT DOWN!** I just kept reading, and reading and reading and reading until finally at the end I was looking for more. The life of V. Ricardo Thomas is a life of hard knocks, hard times, hardness of heart, truth, reality, deliverance and God ultimately getting so much of the glory that He deserves. I guarantee you that if you buy this book, you will not only bless yourself; but you will be able to bless many other people who think that God is too far away to ever reach them, all the way down in a pit and a pig's pen. "I highly without reservation or hesitation, suggest that you purchase a copy of this book, today".*

Darrell V. Freeman, Sr., *Pastor, Author of Investing In Our African American Youth, Counseling In African Communities, and Satan's Commitment to Biblical Counselors.*

ACKNOWLEDGEMENTS

My first thank you is to God who is indeed the ultimate "Promise Keeper," to him be the glory.

To Cynthia, my wife, you came along when I came to my senses and has walked alongside me in the ministry.

To my loving children Tamara, V. Ricardo Jr., Morris, Steven and Dominique, thanks for allowing me back into your lives so that a reconciliation, healing and restoration could take place in our relationship.

Ma Dear, thank you for never giving up on me, even when I was at my lowest.

Latresa Adams and Christenia Wafers without your perseverance this original book or the revised edition would not have been completed. Thanks for your support when I didn't feel like writing.

To my angels, Andrea Ashford and Nickolas A. Dunford, thank you for helping me put together the "There Is Hope..." Seminars which allows this book and other projects to spread the message of hope, help and healing before the two of you went home to be with The Lord. Your belief in me and this project will always stay with me.

Pam Perry of Ministry Marketing Solutions who's expertise and insight has been instrumental in taking this book to the next level.

Dedication

This book is dedicated to the memory of the late Bishop Morris Thomas Sr. my father, who like Abraham staggered not at the promise of God and believed that I would one day live a life that would give God glory. Even though he did not live to see that day, he was fully persuaded that God could perform what he had promised.

Table of Contents

Introduction

Prodigal Son is the true story of my life, V. Ricardo Thomas, Sr., Senior Pastor of Faith Tabernacle Church in Highland Park, Michigan. This gripping book tells how prior to becoming a pastor, I entered into an addictive lifestyle that held me in captivity for over 25 years. I lived a hellish existence. This powerful story is about the redemption, reconciliation and restoration work of Jesus Christ.

In these pages I share with you openly and honestly many of my life's struggles and pains as well as those of my family and friends. Often we don't realize how our lifestyles affect the entire family; children, parents and others. For many years I lived the lowest kind of life, a life of drug addiction, crime, imprisonment, and immorality that was contrary to the will of God.

This book shows a story of hope against all odds and demonstrates the power of the restoration of God. For all of you that have family members, children or loved ones that you know or counsel that struggle with any kind of addictions, whether it be drinking, drugs, gambling, pornography or violence; I want you to know that there is hope and restoration in Jesus Christ. "The Prodigal Son" shows how when I came to my senses and turned to God, he literally took me from the PIT to the PULPIT.

I have been transformed from a peddler of drugs to one that spreads the gospel and a message of hope.

For me to be alive, able to write this book and for you to be reading it to help someone is a miracle and a reason to rejoice and give all the "GLORY TO GOD."

THE PRODIGAL SON
By V. Ricardo Thomas, Sr.

Luke 15:32   But we had to celebrate and be glad, because this brother of yours was dead and is alive again; he was lost and is found.'"   (NIV)

THE PRODIGAL SON ACCORDING TO THE BIBLE

Luke 15:11-32

11   Jesus continued: "There was a man who had two sons.

12   The younger one said to his father, 'Father, give me my share of the estate.' So he divided his property between them.

13   Not long after that, the younger son got together all he had, set off for a distant country and there squandered his wealth in wild living.

14   After he had spent everything, there was a severe famine in that whole country, and he began to be in need.

15   So he went and hired himself out to a citizen of that country, who sent him to his fields to feed pigs.

16   He longed to fill his stoRick McKenzieh with the pods that the pigs were eating, but no one gave him anything.

17   When he came to his senses, he said, 'How many of my father's hired men have food to spare, and here I am starving to death!

18   I will set out and go back to my father and say to him: Father, I have sinned against heaven and against you.

19   I am no longer worthy to be called your son; make me like one of your hired men.'

20   So he got up and went to his father. "But while he was still a long way off, his father saw him and was filled with compassion for him; he ran to his son, threw his arms around him and kissed him.

21   The son said to him, 'Father, I have sinned against heaven and against you. I am no longer worthy to be called your son.'

22   But the father said to his servants, 'Quick! Bring the best robe and put it on him. Put a ring on his finger and sandals on his feet.

23   Bring the fattened calf and kill it. Let's have a feast and celebrate.

24   For this son of mine was dead and is alive again; he was lost and is found.' So they began to celebrate.

25   Meanwhile, the older son was in the field. When he came near the house, he heard music and dancing.

26   So he called one of the servants and asked him what was going on.

27   'Your brother has come, he replied, and your father has killed the fattened calf because he has him back safe and sound.'

28   The older brother became angry and refused to go in. So his father went out and pleaded with him.

29   But he answered his father, 'Look! All these years I've been slaving for you and never disobeyed your orders. Yet you never gave me even a young goat so I could celebrate with my friends.

30   But when this son of yours who has squandered your property with prostitutes comes home, you kill the fattened calf for him!'

31   'My son,' the father said, 'you are always with me, and everything I have is yours.

32   But we had to celebrate and be glad, because this brother of yours was dead and is alive again; he was lost and is found." (NIV)

Chapter 1

The Early Years

I was born in Highland Park, Michigan in 1952. I remember being about three years old when my family moved to my grandparent's house, where we lived on Kendall in Highland Park. Highland Park is a city that is surrounded by Detroit. During that time Highland Park was a clean, middle class suburb, and had one of the best school districts in the country. It was diverse in ethnic makeup and was sustained by the automotive industry. Ford Motor Company's first historical plant that offered workers $5 a day for wages was in Highland Park. Henry Ford believed that workers should be paid a wage that would allow them to purchase the product that they made. He also had the city to put in its own water system and not be depended upon Detroit or another city for water. That way Ford was assured of having cheap water for it's plant. Chrysler Corporation had their world headquarters there as well until the 1990's. Woodward Avenue was vibrant with shoppers patronizing the variety of stores, movie theaters and activities.

People who lived there would say with pride, "Oh, I live in Highland Park," as if it was a badge of honor and indeed it was, then. Similar to people today that say, "I live in Farmington Hills or Troy." However, back then, those places were still pretty much farmland and cow pastures, and Blacks weren't allowed out there. During the 1950's to the 70's Highland Park was one of the elite places to live. It was designated by the U. S. Government as a "Model City"

Every house and apartment building was lived in. Today, Highland Park barely looks the same as it did in the 1950's and 60's. There are many abandoned, burned out houses, debris and weed-filled lots, boarded up storefronts and pothole infested streets. The city looks like the gaped opened mouth of a toothless derelict.

During the 50s, around 1955-57, we were living with Daddy-O and Nana, my paternal grandparents. My father, Morris Sr.; my mother, Betty; myself and Morris Jr., my older brother were all residing there. Morris Jr., (a.k.a. Mo), was four years older and very protective of me and still is today.

We moved into our own home on Doris Street, a couple of streets over from my grandparents, when I was five years old. My younger brother and sister were born while we were living on Doris. My younger brother, Anthony, we called him Tony, is seven years younger than me. He stills lives in that same house to this day. He started his own family with Rose and Anthony Jr. During the summer of 1962, Mo and I were sent to visit my uncle and aunt, Richard and Marie Campbell, who lived in Los Angeles, California. I was ten years old and it was the summer my sister, Lisa, was born. My mother was having major complications during her pregnancy with Lisa. She had a massive tumor, which was growing along side the baby. Mo, Tony and I didn't know it, but she could have died. My mother calls Lisa her "Miracle Baby".

When I was 12 years old, I had gotten into a fight with a friend of ours, Chris Ellis, who lived on Doris Street. He was about three years older than me and much bigger. He was winning hands down and had me on my back hitting me something fierce. Arms were wailing and fists were flying as I covered my faced. Mo had been watching the fight with the other boys on our street. Remember he was protective and when he saw that I was starting to lose the fight, Mo pushed Chris off of me and let me get on top of him. I started throwing in some good punches of my own. The other boys started telling Mo that it wasn't fair. Mo told them, "That's my brother." I never told Mo, but it was that day that I said to myself, "I would always help him if he needed it," and to the best of my ability I have done that.

In my neighborhood everyone knew one another or knew someone that knew someone on my street; everyone knowing everyone is how it was when I was growing up. It

7

was unimaginable then the way things are now, where you have people that live on the same street in the same block and don't know their neighbor's names. We knew every single person on the block, their cousins, aunts, uncles, and even friends when they came over to visit or stay during the summer.

Reflecting on my childhood I grew up without any worries; as Stevie Wonder titled one of his songs, "With A Child's Heart." Playing tag, hide-and-go-seek, kick the can, strikeout, and all the other games that children played before television, videos, Wi-Fi, Wii, cable, Facebook, videos, and text messaging became the source of communication, enjoyment and entertainment.

I played organized little league sports such as baseball and football. It was from our little league that the National Football League player Reggie McKenzie emerged. Reggie went on to star at Highland Park High and the University of Michigan, where he became an All American and College Football Hall of Famer. He was drafted by the Buffalo Bills and was a guard on the line that did all the tremendous blocking for O.J. Simpson. He later ended his career with the Seattle Seahawks. Reggie gives back to the community through the Reggie McKenzie Foundation. The City of Highland Park has renamed the field where we played little league and high school football, as the Reggie McKenzie Field. There were other notable athletes that came out of Highland Park, The Trapp Brothers, John and George who played NBA for Indianapolis, L. A. and the Detroit Pistons. There was also Bobby Joe Hill who played basketball for Texas Western which later became Texas-El Paso, the first college team that had all black starters that won the NCAA championship. The movie "Glory Road" starring Derek Luke as Bobby Joe and Matthew McConaughey as the coach, was based on this championship season.

During the 1960's, there was a train track approximately a few hundred yards behind our house. We used to hop the trains from Hamilton to east of the Woodward Bridge and viaduct to go to the Boy's Club on Ferris Street, or to go ice skating in the winter at Ford Field. In the late 1970's, they built a new high school, which is known as the Highland Park Community High School on the same field where we would ice skate. Growing up, I remember having so much fun with my friends. There was no way that any one could have predicted that my life would turn in the direction that it did. During my school years, I was in the Cub Scouts and I had a newspaper route delivering the Highland Parker newspaper. I started out helping my brother, Mo, with his paper route, delivering the Detroit Times and I saw the extra money he made. I couldn't wait to start making my own money.

My family attended St. Luke African Methodist Episcopal Church on LaBelle in Highland Park, Michigan, where Reverend Walter Crider was Pastor. Bishop Gomez was the presiding Bishop in the Michigan area. Growing up in the church and attending regular services meant going to Sunday school as well as church services, every Sunday. I was fine with that; it was our way of life.

Proverbs 22:6 "Train up a child in the way he should go: and when he is old, he will not depart from it."   (KJV)

My mother and father were both ushers in the church. My mother also sung with the gospel choir at St. Luke A.M.E along with my grandmother, Nana.   My grandfather, Daddy O, attended church every Sunday as well. Mo and I would get a dollar from him some weeks after church, so that we could go to the Highland Park or Grand theaters on Woodward Avenue to see the latest movies. Back then when you went to the movies you were able to see two for the price of admission. Admission was only a quarter, pop was a dime and popcorn was 15 cents, 25 cents if it was buttered.

I remember at the age of five or six when my father stood up in church and acknowledged his "calling" into the ministry. Upon acknowledging his calling, he attended Detroit Bible College which later became known as William Tyndale College. He became ordained in the African Methodist Episcopal (AME) church and went into the ministry, where he received various assignments. His first assignment was as an associate minister at the church we attended. Every year, they would have an annual conference and the leaders would assign where the church ministers and pastors would serve. I remember my father serving in Mount Clemens, Michigan at a small church. While my father served, the membership grew; he was successful and just the kind of young minister that they were looking for to grow struggling churches.

In 1962, my father was given a pastorate in Monroe, Michigan at Carey Chapel AME, the same year my sister, Lisa, was born. Although, my father was pastor in Monroe, our family continued to live in Highland Park, which was approximately 45 minutes to an hour away. This meant driving down to Monroe every Sunday to go to church. In order for the family to get to church at 9:45 a.m. for Sunday school, we had to get up at 6:00 a.m. in the morning to allow all of us time to wash up, eat and get dressed. The boys would usually fall back to sleep in the car on the way driving to Monroe.

I was an altar boy along with Terry Tubbs. We would wear white robes during certain services and assisted the Pastor. We would carry the Bible or help with other religious rites and sacraments, such as communion. I had no idea that over 30 years later I would be ministering as a pastor myself from a pulpit.

11

My mother would prepare most of our Sunday dinners a day early so we could take it with us. She would fry the chicken or warm the roast right after service. If it were summer when the windows were opened, because there was no air conditioning then, we were able to smell the plethora of aromas drifting outside as we played in between services. We ate our Sunday dinners after church in the basement where the church kitchen was located. Every now and then, a member of the church would invite our family to their home for Sunday dinner. After service, we would play around the church or go over to friend's houses, who were also members of the church until it was time for evening service. We spent the entire day on Sundays in Monroe. After a full day, our family would travel back to Highland Park, Michigan and we would get home around 10:00 p.m. This lasted for four years until I reached the age of 14.

My life traveling to Monroe became a norm. I can recall an interesting experience which taught me what "fighting fair" was all about. What I ended up learning was that there was no such thing as "Fighting Fair". Before this experience what I learned when you fought someone was that the two of you would go to blows until one of you quit or one of our friends stopped the fight, because one of you would get the mess beat out of you. There were a few girls in Monroe that were attracted to me and vice versa. We were only 12 or 13 years old, which is usually when children go through their rites of passage and start calling themselves "going with someone" or "going steady," as it was then commonly referred to. Now teenagers have different terms.

Mike, a fellow, who didn't take kindly to the fact that a girl he liked, liked me. This alluded to name calling and he picked a fight with me. Girls, name calling, talking about someone's mama or laying hands on someone were causes worth fighting for back in the day. Youth today want to shoot you for just looking at them wrong. We used to call it "Wreckless Eyeballing"

We were across the street from the church on Almyra Street inside the Fuqua/Tubbs/Woods house. They were a much blended family and members of the church. They had children around the same ages as Mo and I. We played with each other. Mike and I were calling each other names and pushing on each other. Someone suggested that we go outside and fight. I had no problem with that because I loved to fight anyway. Before I went outside, I realized that my shoestring was untied and I didn't want to trip on it while fighting. So I said, "Okay, wait a minute." I kneeled down to tie my shoes. The house where we were had an old coal stove. Mike picked up the iron poker used to stoke the fire and while I was tying my shoes, he started beating me on my back with it. I felt the force of the blows; I thought I was in a dream world. I couldn't believe what was actually happening to me. When it dawned on me that what was happening was real, I went crazy, momentarily lost my mind, got up and whipped his butt. Every since then, I would never even consider fighting a "fair fight". As a matter of fact, I don't even consider it a healthy thing. From that day, whenever I was in a fight I was determined that I would get the first lick in. I would grab a stick, a brick, a knife, a pistol or anything. I made up my mind that I was not going to let anyone get the better of me first; being short in statue didn't matter to me. If I couldn't find something to hit with, then I'd just as soon kick a big guy between the legs, wait for him to bend over, bust his nose open, upper cut, and work the temple.

Mo graduated from Highland Park High School in 1965 and moved to California to live with our uncle and aunt, Richard and Marie, to attend college. The rest of the family went out there and spent the summer, with the exception of my father. Mo was gone and I was the oldest at home. It seemed like that year went by slowly.

The next year was a major change. I entered high school and my parents founded Faith Tabernacle Church of Highland Park, when I was 14 years old. As I mentioned before, my father was ordained in the Methodist church under Reverend Walter Crider, who believed in holiness, the Holy Ghost, and speaking in tongues. Reverend Crider died while my father was pastoring in Monroe, Michigan. During the 1960's there just weren't many people in the A.M.E. church that believed in a Pentecostal experience. The Holy Ghost was something you may get, but you sure didn't express it too often and you had to be dignified when you did. A person would get fanned or ushered out of the sanctuary. Now we call the Holy Ghost the Holy Spirit, which sounds modern in the translation and more acceptable for people to have indwelling in them rather then some Ghost which sounded "spooky" and turned "dignified" people off that did not have full revelation of the Spirit and manifestation of God. This was a period in church history before charismatics and Full Gospel Baptist were growing movements; where Calvary met Pentecost, and the terms "sanctified" and "holiness" were frowned upon by the "dignified" established older denominations. However, the Church of God in Christ was a denomination

15

that was steadily growing and they believed in dancing, speaking in tongues and shouting. Since that time, there has been an outpouring of the Spirit of God on most denominations, while people realize and embrace it. Speaking in tongues, dancing in the Spirit is understood and widely embraced today by many Evangelicals. It wasn't in that time.

My father had been in prayer and was led by God to continue to preach holiness and sanctification. He withdrew from the A.M.E. denomination and started Faith Tabernacle with seven members. People told him that he was crazy, that he would come back, for him to stop the foolishness, etc. Someone asked him if he was sure he was hearing from God. My father told them, "One thing's for sure, I'm going to find out." I can attest today that he was definitely hearing from God. Faith Tabernacle Church of Highland Park is still living and thriving. My grandmother, Nana, joined the church, but my grandfather, Daddy-O, remained at St. Luke A.M.E. When Mo came home from California two years later, he stayed at St. Luke A.M.E also. He didn't want any part of this new way that went against tradition. He was out of high school, had some college, and was allowed to make his own decisions. I was a teenager, and I didn't have a choice as to where I would attend church service. You find so many parents today allowing children to make decision pertaining to worship as if they really understand. All a child wants to do for the most part is play and have fun. They do not want to be disciplined, learn Godly principle or the Bible. As a result, we have the society that we do today.

Faith Tabernacle began in a rented building that was known as a "storefront," located at 108 LaBelle Street in Highland Park, Michigan. Sheets were hung across the windows and the name painted on the glass was "Faith Tabernacle Church - Pastor Morris Thomas, Sr". I would go with my father on Saturday evenings to borrow chairs for the church from Pope Funeral Home that was located on Davison in the Conant Garden neighborhood. We would return the chairs on Sunday night after evening service, so the funeral home would have chairs for Monday services. My father became a Bishop years later after founding other ministries. We stayed in that location for three years. Faith Tabernacle has moved three times since its inception.

The storefront church was such an embarrassment to me. Consequently, I began to rebel against church. I felt that I needed to show my friends that I wasn't any different from them, and I wanted to be cool and accepted.

This is the path that many teenager travel that leads to destruction. Wanting to be accepted but settling for being accepted by the wrong group of people; Other teenagers that are so mixed up, hurt and damaged by their home life of abuse, isolation and disconnection that they

17

begin to form a group that is more dysfunctional than the family that they come from.

That is why today I reach out to so many young people that are hurting, misguided and feeling unloved, so that I can help to mentor them and show them that God does love them and that there are other people and organizations as well that truly care about them. This is why I started Prodigal Son Ministries, in order to spread a message of HOPE.

Chapter 2

Turning Away

Luke 15:13   "Not long after that, the younger son got together all he had, set off for a distant country and there squandered his wealth in wild living. (NIV)

In rebellion, I began to venture off into different things; I began drinking beer and wine. There was an older guy, Martin, who was nine years older than me and lived down the street from us. Martin's nickname was "Tiny" because he was so large; he weighed over 300 pounds. Martin had a younger brother, Mitchell, who was in the Army. Years later, Mitchell started his own construction firm and gave his life to Christ. I talked Martin into allowing me to taste the cheap wine that he and his friends were drinking. They were drinking Orange Driver or Silver Satin, and they would mix it with Kool-Aid. Martin and his friends were some of the athletic guys from Highland Park, who engaged in wild behavior. Some members of this group formed a baseball team and called themselves "Wine Nine," and played in a summer league that many   "Parkers" which is what the residents of Highland Park referred to themselves as, attended in large numbers.

Eventually, the alcohol wasn't enough, and, at the

age of 15, I tried smoking marijuana, which had multiple effects on me. My friends and I would be silly and would laugh at anything and everything. Sometimes, we thought we were real deep and philosophical, and would discuss everything we could think of. I continued smoking weed even after I started using heroin and cocaine, until I stopped getting high altogether. One of the insane things that teenagers think when they're smoking marijuana is that no one else smells it on them or think no one knows what they are doing. The smell gets in your clothes, in your hair and in your pores. Once, my parents were away from home, I had smoked weed at the back door and thought the smoke had blown outside. Evidently, some smoke had blown back into the house, because when my parents came home, my father asked, "What's that I smell?" He said it smelled like burnt rope. He didn't come right out and accuse me or ask if I was smoking weed. So, I just answered and said, "I don't smell anything." **Dope will make you do stupid things.**

My drinking continued throughout high school. Today, I am not surprised or shocked when I read how prevalent and widespread drugs, alcohol and sex are in the high schools. That is the reason why there are so many sexually transmitted disease cases on the rise. My drink of choice in the ninth and tenth grade was Gin, either Seagrams or Booths. My mellow, Lanny's, was Black Bull scotch. We would make sure that we each had a pint before the high school basketball games or special events, along with a couple of joints. There were quite a few students who were getting high on a regular basis, as well as others that would get high on the weekends, or when our sports teams were playing against other schools.

During the summer of 1968, at the age of 16, I went on a trip around the United States sponsored by my high school. It was referred to as a traveling classroom and we received credits for social studies and history. There were about 15 male students and three chaperones. One of the chaperones was a teacher and the other two were student teachers. We all traveled in three station wagons. This trip birthed a desire in me to travel; to see more of the world, more than Detroit, Michigan.

It was amazing that not one of us went to jail on that trip. Some of us stole and committed B&Es (Breaking and Entering) in various cities and states along the way on our trip. We smoked weed and drank beer, as well. As a matter of fact, I came home with more money than when I left. We went to Mackinaw, Michigan; Green Bay, Wisconsin; Minneapolis - St. Paul, Minnesota; Rapid City, South Dakota; Salt Lake City, Utah; Las Vegas, Nevada; Waco, Texas; Denver and Colorado Springs, Colorado; Des Moines, Iowa; and Chicago, Illinois.

I bought a car with the money that I made while on

the trip, along with money from a safe that Lanny and I took from a janitorial service that we had broken into. When I was 16, I had my own automobile in high school. You couldn't tell me that I wasn't living large and that I wasn't a baller and big shot caller. The funny thing about it was that I couldn't park the car on my street, because I couldn't let my father know I had it. If he knew that I had a car with no legal means to get it, I don't know what he might have done to me. It was 1968 and the car was a 1967 yellow Thunderbird convertible that I bought from my cousin, JoAnn's husband, Verne. He was hooked up in all kinds of illegal activities, one of which was a stolen car ring. It entailed stealing cars, tagging and resaling them. Tagging consisted of changing the Vehicle Identification Number, which is commonly known as the VIN number. First, purchase a wrecked car and obtain the title for it from the Secretary of State. Second, steal an identical model of car and take the VIN tags off of the wreck, whether it was working or not, and put the numbers on the stolen car. If stopped by the police, the driver had legitimate papers for the car. I eventually got another car from Verne the same way, and I was able to keep it until the spring of 1969. It needed repairs, and I was not able to get it fixed. I was trying to focus on school and take care of my drug habit. I couldn't ask my father to take a look at it and tell me what he thought was wrong with it, because I knew it was stolen.

Verne was also into drugs and fencing, which was buying & selling stolen property. You name it, Verne was into it. He schooled me on many of my criminal enterprises. I B&E'd into businesses and took whatever wasn't nailed down, such as IBM electric typewriters, adding machines, radios, appliances and other miscellaneous items that I thought would be of value. Computers weren't as compact, popular and mass-produced as they are now. If so, I would have been taking them as well. Verne was just one of my fences. He's the one that taught me about the value of checks. He would offer me a dollar or two for every blank check I brought him. Whenever I would break into a business, I would take a bunch of commercial checks out of the bottom of the stack of the package if there was only one or the last box if they had plenty, so they wouldn't notice it right away. It only took me a couple of times of selling them to Verne, to figure the math out myself. He would have someone cash one check and get all of his money back. The rest of the money would be profit or you could just sell the blank checks for a price higher than what you paid for them. I filed this information away in my mind and would put it to use some years later when I formed my own "paper hanging" crew. "Hanging paper" was the term used for cashing checks that didn't belong to you. The criminal and judicial system calls it Uttering and Publishing and it can get you 14 years in the penitentiary.

In the fall of 1968, when I returned from the trip, I started using heroin. When I started using heroin, my drinking sharply declined. I remember when I first used heroin it was in the first Thunderbird that I had. I remember sitting in my car with my friend, Doris Davidson, who grew up with me on Doris. We were sitting in the car and getting ready to do a B&E at the Stage Delicatessen resturant in Oak Park. I had worked there briefly the summer before as a dishwasher for a couple of weeks while a friend of mine was on vacation. We were planning on stealing the safe after a busy weekend. People were still in the building, so Doris suggested that we go and get some **penny caps (small red gelatin capsules)** of "Boy" (a slang name for heroin) to pass the time away. They called them penny caps back then because they cost a dollar a piece. I wanted to be cool with him. Actually, when I think about it, I wanted to be accepted; he was my boy. I agreed and we went and copped a few penny caps, sat in my car and snorted the dope.

We drove to a drug house in the neighborhood and he went in to cop (purchase the drugs). Afterwards, we drove the car elsewhere and he took out the penny caps. He opened them up and emptied the powder on a book. We used whatever we could find -- a book, piece of paper, album covers, mirrors, etc. Sometimes we used a card or a razor blade to chop it up and put it into lines. We also used a small straw or a rolled dollar bill as a pathway to sniff the dope in our nose. Sometimes we would keep it in a pile and use the corner of the card to scoop the dope and snort it.

Doris put dope on the card and put it to my nose for me to snort. "Make sure you inhale it and DON'T!! breathe out or you'll blow the dope away," he told me. He was adamant when he told me and I never forgot that rule. "Never waste the dope." After a few hits, I started to feel sick and nauseated. Doris suggested that we go and buy a "Red Pop." He said that it would increase the high. I drank the pop and afterwards I began to throw up. The first time a person does heroin, gets nauseated and throws up, the high seems to magnify. We went over to my cousin, JoAnn's house. We sat there, half looking at television, talking with her whenever she came into the room; we nodded the rest of the night. Needless to say, there was no B&E job pulled that night.

That was my very first experience with hard drugs. A feeling of euphoria overtook me and I floated with it. I rode the waves of drifting in and out of consciousness for a significant period of time. The first high on heroin was like no other in the world, and it could not be surpassed by any feeling that existed. I didn't realize until 14 years later that I would find a higher level when I began to freebase cocaine and smoke crack.

I didn't know then that I was falling into a trap that would hold me captive for a long time. I didn't stop using heroin until 19 years later, but I continued to use cocaine. There was an era of forced abstinence from heroin when I went to prison for two years. It wasn't that I could not score, because it was available in the penal system; it was just too expensive. I was satisfied with selling and smoking weed and having an occasional drink while I was incarcerated. I knew I would not get sick if I didn't have them, like I would if I had a heroin habit in jail and couldn't cop.

One of the dangers and pitfalls of sin that I always say is that "It will take you further than you plan on going, keep you longer than you planned on staying, and cost you more than what you are willing to spend."

Heroin was so enticing in the 60s, especially to young Black men who had a void in their lives. Heroin would fill the empty places and soothe all the hurts and scars remaining from growing up. It seemed as if it gave me a sense of coolness and acceptance by others, which I considered hip. To this day, some people believe the heroin that flooded the United States in the 1960s was distributed with the tacit approval of the government. There was so much unrest and civil disturbance in all of the major urban cities such as Detroit, Chicago, Los Angeles, Cleveland , New York and Washington DC. Heroin was a means of pacifying and incapacitating many disenfranchised, violent, emotional, angry and militant young Black men.

Heroin is the "Master Con Man." It entices with a sense or belief of belonging to the in crowd. However, upon awakening, one day you find that you have been deceived, tricked, bamboozled and that in reality you're an outcast to society. You realized that no one wants to socialize with drug addicts but other addicts. The strongest of people become slaves when hooked on drugs.

That day was the beginning for me snorting heroin and I enjoyed it. It became a regular activity in my life. First, I would only indulge on the weekends but before I knew it, I was "using" drugs during the week as well. Before long, I was hooked and had a habit and didn't even realize it.

One day, while riding in a car with some other guys that I went to school with, I began telling my friend, Rick McKenzie that I had been feeling very sick all day. "Rick ," I said, "I've been so sick today. I've been throwing up yellow stuff." Rick McKenzie told me, "Man, you're bogue." I said, "bogue, what do you mean bogue"? He said, "Have you had a blow today?" (Blow was a street term for getting high on drugs.) "A blow," I said, "naw, I didn't feel like I wanted to get high today." He said, "Let's go around the corner and get a blow." We went around the corner and copped a blow. I immediately snorted and to my amazement, I wasn't sick any longer. Rick McKenzie explained to me that my system was used to having some dope on a regular basis and when I didn't supply it, my body would react as such. I would get sick, vomiting, bones aching, sweating, and having chills and diarrhea. This is when I first recognized that I had a heroin habit. From that day forward, I had to have it, so that I wouldn't be sick. I was in my junior year in high school, 16 years old, and a heroin addict. The amazing thing is that I was still maintaining decent school grades. I was a functional, society-pleasing student; yet, I was a closet drug user.

Chapter 3

Feeding The Monkey

I was in high school with a heroin habit and that meant that I needed money on a regular basis. I had a responsibility, which was to keep the monkey on my back fed. When an appetite is fed, it has a tendency to grow. I didn't realize that the monkey would grow into a giant gorilla.

I started increasing my B&Es and soon had to go beyond local businesses. I looked for businesses in other industrial areas. I felt it was too dangerous to B&E private homes. Although, I did go on several jobs when it was set up and checked out in advance. I would not go in cold, which meant going in without prior planning. I could get busted by nosey neighbors or killed, because the people might return home. I had friends that had to fight with the owners of houses once inside.

I remember one guy in particular, Marvin, he was shot in the butt while escaping from a house going out a window. Some guys were even bold enough to do what we called "creeping." They would go in someone's house while they were sleeping and steal their valuables. This took more nerve than I had in me. I decided to stick with business establishments, which was good money at the time and I didn't have to fake nerves of steel when it came to doing something that to me was past insanity.

In the spring of 1969 my car was stolen by my cousin, Verne. This was the car that I couldn't get fixed at the time. He saw it parked in front of Lanny's house and decided he needed it. He told Lanny that I sent him to get it. Lanny was unsuspecting and believed Verne was on the up and up, gave him the keys. I paid him back for that and some later on. I didn't have a car then, so I had to use my father's. Bishop had a 1965 black Cadillac. One thing my father always taught us was not to ever worship a car. It could be a Lincoln or Cadillac but to him it was just a car. It may be expensive, but it's only material possession. One of his favorite sayings was "a poor ride is better than a proud walk". He taught us to ride a hoopdie, which was an old beat up car, just as proud as a luxury, because it was yours. He also pointed out to me that a person with a car and money will always have plenty of people hanging around them. You will find out who your real friends are and who are just around for your ride and money. If my siblings or I, were responsible when driving the car, we were allowed to drive whatever car the family had. However, no drinking or smoking was allowed in his car. One of the things that I feared the most was what my father would do to me if he found out I had used his car on a B&E. In a manner of speaking, I was more terrified of what my betrayal of his trust would do to him than being busted by the police.

The first time that I was arrested other than juvenile, was for breaking into Harry Thomas Clothiers, which was a top of the line men's store on Seven Mile and Sussex. Needless to say, I was driving Bishop's car and after this incident, I was grounded from using the family car for a while. This job started out with me, Derrick, who grew up on Doris, Ronald and Johnny. After I picked everyone up, Ronald got cold feet and said his horoscope predicted something bad would happen that day. He got out the car by Palmer Park and caught the bus back home. We laughed at him and called him scared, but he ended up having the last laugh.

When we were at the store, Derrick and I went in through the roof skylight. Derrick was supposed to have cased the place out, but he didn't do a good enough job because a silent alarm went off. We were piling clothes up by the door when we noticed police cars pulling in front. We immediately tried to find a place to hide. I hid behind a clothes rack against the wall while the police waited for the manager to come and let them into the store. The police searched for about half an hour and thought that we had gone back out through the skylight. One of the police officers decided to go through the store once more, and when he did I was busted. I think I scared him more than he scared me. God was protecting me, even then, because he didn't have his pistol drawn. I could have been shot. The way he jumped backed I could tell that he was startled. They never found Derrick. Johnny was arrested walking down the street. I guess he just looked suspicious. Once we were at the precinct, they kept Johnny. I was sent to the juvenile center because I was only 16 years old at the time. The juvenile center where I went is known as the James Lincoln Juvenile center today. It is named in memory of the Judge that presided over it for many years.

A few days later, they found out that Derrick was in on the job also because after the police left, he broke out a window to escape. He went down the street from the store and stole something out of a garage. He left his fingerprints inside the clothing store and in the garage. A good attorney could have argued that the prints in the store could have been there for some time. His prints already were on file because he had a previous police record, so they issued a warrant for his arrest.

The next morning, they turned me over into the custody of my father. The detectives told me that I was to testify against Derrick and Johnny when the case went to trial. Once the case went to trial, I told the judge that I was acting alone and that the only reason that I agreed to testify in the first place was because the detectives had scared me into doing it. I told the court that they told me that I would never go to college with a record. I told the judge, "Misery loves company your Honor, but with my father being a pastor and all, I know it's not right to lie and say someone was with me when they weren't." I was lying through my teeth, even then.

The Prosecutor asked my father to come in from waiting in the hallway. He asked me if I would say the same thing, that I just said, in front of my father, which I did with a straight face. The judge dismissed the case against Derrick and Johnny. As I was leaving the witness stand, the judge said, "Hold it right there." He said, "Young man, if there was any way that I could hold you for contempt of court or perjury, I would, because I know without a doubt that you are lying. I hope for your sake that you never come before this bench again. Reverend Thomas, please have a talk with your son, before it's too late."

As we were riding home, my father told me that I took a heck of a chance on the stand lying to cover up for someone, who, if the shoe was on the other foot, would have given me up. He said, "Rick, the road that you are on right now, you'd better get off of it. The guys that you are hanging out with are only going to take you down, and you will end up dead or going to the penitentiary like your uncles, Bud and Ray." In most African American families there is always an uncle, brother, cousin or some other relative that has been or is in prison. Most often families don't talk about them, as if they will go away. However, it is a reality of life. My father went on to say, "If you go to Jackson", which is the name of the city that the State Penitentiary of Southern Michigan was located in, "You will be given a number and that number will stay with you for the rest of your life." His words became a reality almost 12 years later. I ended up receiving such a number when I went to Jackson on a drug case years later.

Chapter 4

"Steal From My Family, Who Me?"

After I had been using drugs for a while, I would listen to other users say, "I would never steal from my family, I don't need it that bad." I would just tell them, "Just keep on using and you will be surprised what you will end up doing." I used to say the same thing when I first started using. It was so easy to cop and it didn't cost that much when I first started. As I mentioned earlier, when I started using heroin, we bought penny caps that cost a dollar a piece.

The first time I stole from my family, it was from my grandmother. She stayed a couple of streets over from us on Kendall Street. I would always go over to my grandmother's house to visit or do odds and ends jobs and my grandmother would pay me. My grandfather had passed away the previous year. One day, I looked in a drawer in the living room table for something and I saw her checkbook. I took a couple of checks from the back of her checkbook, thinking it would be a long time before she noticed that they were gone. I forged her signature and went to the bank and cashed the check. It was so easy that I went the next day and cashed the other one. Forgery was something I would become very good at when I started hanging paper on a regular basis; I wasn't knowledgeable enough at this time to use false identification, which I did when I led my own paper hanging stable (group of women) and crew (group of men).

I was at home and my father called me from my grandmother's house and told me to come over there. This was about two months after I had cashed the checks. As a matter of fact, I had forgotten all about it. I walked in to Nana's house and my father was sitting in the living room with Nana. "Explain these to me" he said, as he threw the two canceled checks down onto the table. They seemed to leap off the table and slap me in my face. I just stood there for what felt like eternity, as I looked back and forth at Nana with tears streaming down her face and my father with a look of hurt and disgust. All I could think of at that time was, "God, Nana knows I'm on drugs."

When those that you love and hold you in high esteem find out that you're on dope, it's a crushing feeling. Dope fiends, while developing a callous heart and mindset, will easily make the statement, "This is my life and I'm going to live it my way." At first feeling and believing that they are not hurting anyone but themselves. But then they begin to disgust themselves for the pain they inflict on loved ones. This is why the hardness of the heart develops; it stops the addict from feeling the pain; personal pain and the pain that they inflict on others. The drugs help to medicate the pain and, therefore, the perpetual use and psychological dependency, aside from the physical dependency, develops.

Finally, my father snapped me back to the moment. "Did you hear what I said? Why did you steal from Mama?" I still couldn't admit to him and especially in front of Nana, that I was hooked on dope; although, he had asked me previously on several occasions. He had even stated that he thought I was on drugs because of my behavior. I, like many others, lied and denied it. I just used the same old stupid answer that kids give, "I don't know why I did it." He told me in no uncertain terms that if I was to ever steal from his mama again that he would kill me. He placed a primal fear in me. I was afraid to find out if he meant it literally or figuratively, so I never stole from her again. He made up a list of things that I had to do around her house to pay her back. In addition, he added punitive work.

Twenty years later, after my father died, I would end up stealing checks from my own mother. This was one of the incidents that led me to the decision to seek serious treatment. My mother had to go to the bank and have them to red-flag her account. The bank was instructed not to cash anything with my name on it. I found this out after I stopped using and did some work for her. She had written me a check; I went to the bank to cash it. The bank informed me that they could not cash any checks with my name on it from my mother's account. She had to come to the bank and sign papers to have the red-flag lifted. With family members, I used my own name on checks because it was convenient and I felt that they wouldn't press charges against me. Drug addicts are users. They use not only drugs but they will use people, places, and situations all to their advantage and immediate gratification. An addict will deal with the consequences later because of the shady decisions that are made in a moment of need for drugs. The internal pain that is felt afterwards when family and friends look at you with disgust and disbelief hurts so much that more drugs are sought to ease the pain and make you forget how far you have sunk in the cesspool of life.

I would steal blow fare (money) off my parent's dresser, out of their drawers, under their mattress or in purses or wallets. It all had my name on it as far as I was concerned. I even had the nerve, in the beginning, to feel good about myself because I wouldn't take all of the money that was lying out or put away; I would leave some. When confronted, I would always lie, except with those checks, I couldn't deny. After all, they had my signature on them.

People used to comment to my mother about all the gold chains that she wore on her neck and wrist. She didn't have the heart to tell them she wore all of her jewelry because if she didn't wear it all, I would most likely steal it. When I grew older and left home, I was not allowed in the house unless someone else was there. My keys to the house were taken away. It had gotten to the point that I was only allowed to come by to visit. I would take my father's rifles and pawn them, because I knew he wouldn't be looking for them until deer hunting season in November. I can't even imagine all the hurt and pain that I put my family through. Sometimes when I have flashbacks, I shutter to think that I was so far gone.

Chapter 5

Mainlining

I began to realize that those that shot their dope intravenously were getting higher and that their high lasted longer. I wanted to experience that kind of high. It was during the spring of 1969 when I started shooting dope in my veins; the high was instantaneous. Back then, we didn't use syringes as we began to use later. We made syringes with a Maurine eyedropper, which had a rubber band around the black bulb part for an airtight fit and a hypodermic needle.

The first time I shot up, I was in a dope house that a friend of mine, Clyde Beatty, had on Hamilton and Waverly. I told him that I was ready to shoot up and he was willing to oblige me. Clyde opened the caps of heroin, dumped the contents in a metal pop bottle cap, which we called a cooker. A cooker could be a bottle cap, a metal spoon or the metal lid off a jar. He then placed some water in it, struck matches and held them under the cap to cook the dope. Once it began to bubble, it was ready. He took a small piece of cotton and rolled it up in between his fingers and dropped it into the cooker. Clyde drew up the dope into the dropper through the cotton, which acted as a filter to make sure there was no debris of any kind that would get into the syringe and my blood system. Next, he took the syringe, held it upside down and thumped it to make sure there were no air pockets in it. An air pocket can travel through the veins, reach the heart, and it can be fatal. He tied my arm with a stocking to make my veins more visible. Once this was done, he thumped the needle into my vein and immediately a gush of blood began to seep into the dropper. He told me that I had a hit. A hit is when the needle goes into the vein clean. Therefore, the dope goes into the system better and not into surrounding tissue or muscle, which causes people to swell and develop abscesses. The abscesses were caused by the quinine that we used to cut the heroin, which caused the breakdown of the tissue. Eventually, every addict that shoots dope, veins start to collapse from extensive drug use. It becomes difficult to get a good hit. Subsequently, the addict shoots the dope anyway and anywhere, and pays the consequences later.

Apparently, the entire process must have put me in a trance because this image was etched in my mind. I remembered each step so that I could be able to shoot myself up without the help of anyone. Soon after, I started doing just that, what is commonly known in the drug world as "mainlining." In the drug world, we did "skin-popping," which was taking a higher grade of heroin without quinine and shooting it into the muscle tissue. When I would go to cop (buy drugs) with the fellas, I would usually buy myself a few extra caps to shoot up later.

We would skip school to go over to someone's house, whose parents worked and wouldn't be at home, so we could get high. We would have the dope on an album cover or mirror passing it around to get a snort. Once I saw they were starting to get high and nod, I would slip off and go into the bathroom and shoot up.

One day my friend, Lanny, busted in the bathroom on me. He thought that I might have been stealing some of the guy's dope and snorting it myself. "Aw man Rick, what you doing?" he asked me. "What does it look like I'm doing? I'm shooting dope. Go on out and I'll talk to you about it later. They're going to be suspicious with us both gone. Tell them that I'm on the toilet and will be down in a minute." He told me that he had been watching my moves for about a week and decided to see what was up. It didn't take long to shoot dope when I first started because my veins were big and at this point I knew what I was doing. About five or ten minutes later, I would be back with the fellas nodding and scratching. The itching and scratching was a result of the quinine in the dope. During this time, heroin was cut with quinine and lactose. In the 1970s, the dealers, including myself, would start to use Dormaine, a sleeping capsule to add to heroin.

Lanny soon followed my lead in shooting dope. Grady was already shooting up. As a matter of fact, he would make extra money in the evening by working in Clyde's joint. We would snort with the fellas during the day, so we would not warrant suspicion by the two of us going to the bathroom, because Lanny couldn't hit himself then. In the evenings, we would go down on 12th Street and cop and do up. 12th street was like Broadway is to the theater district in New York. The actual theaters are not on Broadway, but on the streets off of Broadway. So when we said we were going down on 12th to cop, we would go to the different streets off of 12th such as Blaine, Philadelphia, Gladstone, and Pingree; "in the hood."

We would admire the pimps and players that hung around the Astor, Chit-Chat Lounge, Bamboo Bar and other watering holes and eating establishments in the area. One of the places that we would cop at was Chicago Red's on Pingree. We loved to go there in the evenings and listen to the stories that Red would tell us about the different jazz artists that he knew back in Chicago and here in Detroit; some of them shot dope themselves. When we found out that Charlie Parker and Billie Holiday shot dope, we just knew we were in good company. The young fools that we were, if we only knew the slippery road to hell that we were already sliding on, we would've jumped off; but, then again, we were hooked.

Remembering the infatuation that I had with the lifestyle, I understand the mindset of youth and how it gets ingrained into their lifestyle even today, the way they gravitate towards the thug life; gansta rappers and the like. Wearing their pants below their butts because it is a fashion statement, yet not understanding that there aren't jobs available for boys that need to use their hands and can't because they have to keep reaching down to pull their pants up.   They think because they look like Lil Wayne, somebody is gonna drop a big check in their hand. It ain't happening. There is no difference, the same way that we thought we were hip and cool back then, they do too. If only more of us, who have survived, would tell them, we may be successful in saving some lives. If we all could just reach one, it would make a world of difference. As the saying goes, "Each one, reach one."

In order to get to Chicago Red's joint, we had to walk around to the back of the building and go down some stairs, because he was in the basement. This was the beginning of the many dangerous routes that I would travel to cop some drugs; walking down alleys, through dark corridors with little or no lighting, up flights of stairs with all sorts of robbers, thieves, killers and common riff raff. These are the type of circumstances that a person who uses drugs consider to be a minor inconvenience and chance that has to be taken. Years later, I would find myself sticking my hard hustled money through a slot or hole in a door, not seeing whom I would be copping from, and hope that they would send my dope back out through the hole. The face-to-face copping days in dope houses had almost come to an end; thanks to the rash of stick-ups and killings of people that worked in dope houses in the late 60's and the 70's.

Lanny and I continued to shoot dope until the summer of 1969, and then we weaned ourselves off. We did this because we needed to get in shape for the upcoming high school football season. We both played on the varsity team and I would be the starting quarterback that year. Lanny was all-league and a very good offensive guard and defensive linebacker. We stayed clean all of six weeks, until the middle of July.

A week or so before the season practices were to begin, my friend "O" told us about how good the dope was down on 12th Street. We forgot all about our vow to get into shape and hurried down to cop. After copping, we went to Lanny's house on LaBelle Street to shoot up, which by the way was across the street from our church, Faith Tabernacle in Highland Park. Lanny had a bedroom on the third floor of his house, where we hung out. "O" had finished and started nodding right away. I was starting to do mine at this time. Lanny was waiting until I was done because he didn't have his own works (this is what we called the syringe, cooker and tie) at that time. Back then, HIV and AIDS hadn't come on the scene and it was a common practice for addicts to share needles and any other drug paraphernalia. There were, however, cases of people contracting jaundice or hepatitis from each other.

I remember getting the hit and starting to squeeze the bulb on the syringe to push the dope into my vein. It had an immediate effect and I started to tell Lanny how good it was and the next thing I remembered, I was waking up in the back seat of a car. I overdosed (OD'd) for the _first_ time, which I understood afterwards. I fell flat on my face on the floor. Lanny and "O" went into a panic at first. Lanny picked me up and slung me over his shoulder and carried me down three flights of stairs. His sister came out of her bedroom on the second floor wandering what was going on. Lanny's parents had company over and they were sitting in the living room and dining room. They were startled to see him running down the stairs carrying me, and "O" was following right behind, which must have been a sight.

Lanny threw me in the back seat of my father's car and "O" jumped up front with him. Later, Lanny told me, he didn't know what to do at that point. He said he drove up to Hamilton and started toward my brother, Mo's, apartment on Webb. He said that as he was driving down Hamilton and that all he could think of was to start praying, and that is what he did. Just before the car reached Webb, I started coughing and regaining consciousness. The three of us knew that it was the hand of God because they didn't perform CPR, walk me around or perform any other measures. The Bible tells us in Romans 5:8 *"But God commendeth his love toward us, in that, while we were yet sinners, Christ died for us."* (KJV) I know from experience that this is true, because while I was yet caught up in the drug lifestyle, God loved me so much that he didn't let me die.

This was the first of five times that I overdosed. One time I was at my cousin, JoAnn's, apartment. Another time, I was at a joint I was running on Oakland Street, located in an area commonly known as the North End. There was also the time I overdosed in my parent's house, which was one of those times that parents and loved ones of drug addicts talk about when you have pushed them over the edge. I imagine this incident was beyond anything that my parents could have ever imagined happening to them; to actually experience their child, me, OD and not knowing if I was going to live or die.

At this point in my life I had developed a routine. I would come home, usually late at night after copping my last blow for the day. Every one would be asleep, my father, mother, Tony and Lisa. During this period, Mo had already moved out and had his own place. I would go in the bathroom, on the first floor and shoot my dope, clean up, and sit at the kitchen table and nod until my mother would come downstairs and send me to bed before my father would find me at the kitchen table, high. One particular night I had copped, but the guy whom I copped from, his woman had mixed up the bags. One bag had "P" in it, which was the strong stuff and the other had a cut on it. I ended up with a spoon of the strong stuff.

I went about my usual routine and went in the bathroom to shoot up. I couldn't find my cooker, so I used one of my mother's tablespoons to cook up my dope. This caused the spoon to turn black on the bottom and was difficult to clean. I didn't care, I had to get high. I remembered shooting the dope in. The next thing I knew, my father was holding me up and walking me around Hackett Field which was later renamed Reggie McKenzie Field, who went on to star in the National Football League.

I found out the next day that my mother had come downstairs as usual, but I wasn't at the kitchen table. She looked outside and saw the Cadillac in the driveway so she knew that I had come home. She looked in my room. I wasn't in the bed. She looked in the basement but I wasn't down there. Finally, while she was standing by the bathroom door, she heard my erratic and guttural breathing. She said it sounded like a death rattle and it frightened her almost to death. She was frozen for a moment, just staring at the closed door, praying that I hadn't locked it. When she opened the door, I was slumped on the floor with the spike (needle) still in my hand. It had come out of my arm when I fell. Blood was on the floor and my arm. The spoon, matches and bag were scattered on the floor from the fall. She tried to lift me up but was unable to move me by herself, so she called my father.

When I came to myself, I could hear Bishop, who was constantly talking to me. He ended up walking me down to McKenzie Field, talking to me all of the time. "Stay awake now Rick, keep walking. You okay? Do you think you have to go to the hospital?" He walked me back home where he and my mother gave me coffee and made sure that I was okay.

Through my drugged filled state I was still able to see the love, concern, compassion and even the hurt that was on their faces as we sat at the kitchen table that night. Deep inside, not wanting to ever see that hurt again yet feeling somewhat compelled to keep living the painful and shameful life that I was caught up in.

The unconditional love of a parent was hard for me to understand. I wanted it, but I still couldn't understand it. Not until I had children of my own.

Chapter 6

Senior Year

In the fall of 1969, the beginning of my senior year in high school, I was elected the Class President. I was very popular and I knew just about everyone in the school; the scholarly, the not so scholarly, as well as the riff raff and thugs. I could converse and assimilate with whatever group I happened to be with. Both groups knew it and found this amazing. I guess it was because it wasn't an act for me. I felt at home and comfortable talking about current events on a local, national or an international level, as well as talking about criminal activity. I wasn't a National Honor student but I managed to be one of the top students of my class. The scholarly group knew I was using drugs. As a matter of fact, many of them smoked a little weed every now and then, and took a drink on the weekends at games and parties. They didn't have a clue that in my briefcase, I sometimes had a pistol, B&E tools and/or my works to shoot dope. If only they had known the extent to which I was involved in drugs and the secretive criminal life that I lived, they would have shunned me like the plague. Although, it came natural for me to live two lifestyles, it wasn't always easy to maintain.

Lanny and I had formed a Jazz Club. I was also the quarterback of the varsity football team, which had the best season at Highland Park High in 17 years. There were probably seven or eight of us on the team using drugs daily.

It was during my senior year that Arthur Blackwell introduced me to golf. His father was the Mayor of Highland Park, Michigan at the time. Arthur went on to become Chairman of the Wayne County Commissioners and a very successful businessman in the Detroit area. Arthur was appointed by Governor Jennifer Granholm to be the Emergency Financial Manager for the City of Highland Park after it fell into bankruptcy years later. I graduated with his sister, June, who is currently a judge in the Wayne County Judicial System. She and I still remain good friends. I started playing golf on the school team. When I saw that people from all walks of life, from factory workers to business people and dignitaries on the golf course, I knew this was somewhere that I could easily be comfortable. However, I sold my clubs and quit playing when the drugs completely took over my life. I eventually started back playing golf again 20 years later. Now, I play wherever I travel, all over the world.

(Photographed: Arthur Blackwell, V. Ricardo Thomas, Cornell Burris.)

There was a group of us, Grady, Posse, Rufus, Bruce and myself that began to steal tape decks out of cars. We would come to school and decide who would go out that particular day. We had rotating days, so if one of us had to take a test or could not afford to miss a certain class, that person would stay in school and the rest of us would go out stealing. It was easy for me because I had most of my prerequisites completed to graduate and only had two classes to take my senior year. The guy that stayed behind would still get blow fare for the day and a few dollars to put in his pocket, but no way would he get an equal split. After all, we that went out were taking the chance of getting busted by the police.

Our main feasting grounds, as we called the areas we would target, were the college campuses in the area. Wayne State University, University of Detroit, Lawrence Institute of Technology, Henry Ford Community College,

Schoolcraft and Marygrove College. Our first fence was Mitchell Hampton's ex- brother-in-law, Buck. Buck owned a business called the "The Shack" on Livernois, at Bourke. He sold and installed tape players in cars. He would pay us a set fee of two dollars per 8-track tape and $15 to $25 for the tape deck, depending on the model. During this time the new thing that was upcoming was cassette decks and tapes, which demanded a higher price. As we continued to steal, we discovered the buying habits of the public. Eventually, more and more people were converting to cassette decks and the 8-track players were starting to become obsolete. Much like today, as DVD players are replacing VHS tape cassettes in homes and CD's and MP3 players have begun to replace cassette tapes and record albums.

We began to bring Buck so much merchandise that he couldn't handle it all and he wanted to start giving us less money, so we had to start finding new fences. We were learning the business, the principles of supply and demand. We learned that there was a larger market for the tapes of the white artists than the blacks. Before we found that out, we would throw the white artist tapes away because they didn't sell in the hood. Once we found white (Caucasian) fences, we couldn't sell the tapes fast enough. The profit was in volume then and the price per tape dropped slightly. The average car was good for twenty

53

tapes and a player. With the tape player, this would average out to about $75 per car that we hit. So if we hit five to ten cars each time we went out, which we did 2 or 3 times a week, we did pretty good financially. We had enough money to maintain our habits and still keep money in our pockets. I loved to dress nice, so I would buy clothes. As a matter of fact, the first suit that I had tailored made was while I was in high school.

The tool of the trade was a large briefcase, so we looked like college students, but inside we had long screwdrivers that slid into windows to pop up the locks in the cars we had tools to dismantle the tape decks. This was all before they started snatching the decks out of the dashboard; very few cars had alarms then. It was probably because of the increasing thefts of tape decks that caused the increase in car alarms on college campuses. Once we were inside the car, we would load the tape deck and the tapes, if they weren't in a case, into the briefcases and unload them into the trunk of whoever's car we were riding in.

I learned in my senior year of high school that I was not too old for a whipping or, in my case, a beating. You hear parents tell their children, "Child I brought you into this world and I'll take you out of it." Well on this particular day, I thought that my father was going to make that cliché a reality. Daddy had already warned me on several occasions not to bring dope or any of my foolishness into the house. He said it was God's house, as well as theirs, and I was going to respect it or get out.

One morning after we had gone stealing, I stored some of the stuff at my house in the den. The den was the place that I would entertain my friends. There was a record player, desk, couch and a couple of chairs on which we would lounge. I put the tape players in the drawers of the desk. My father was out delivering mail for the Post Office. He was a working pastor, not full time because the church was just starting and could not afford to pay him a salary to run the ministry full time. We left the house with some of the tape players and the tapes to go and sell and cop us some dope. While we were gone, my father came home and saw the tape players that we left behind in the desk drawers. He waited a while for me to come home but I didn't come right back. So he went back to work.

In the meantime, we sold everything that we had and the fence wanted more. We went back to my house to get the other merchandise to sell to him. After we sold everything else we copped some dope then went to my house to get high. We had gotten high and there were about five of us just lounging in the den, when my father walked in the house. He came barreling in the room and snatched all the drawers of the desk out; but they were empty by this time. We were so high that we only half came out of our nods. "Where are those tape players that were in here earlier? Were they stolen? I told you don't bring any of your stolen stuff in my house." As I mentioned before, dope will have you do and say some of the dumbest things. I was so high that I blurted out to my father, "Yeah, they were stolen. What do you think?" I must have lost the little sense I still had left. He said, "Fellas, y'all better leave. Rick, I'm about to kick your a--". I was startled. This made me come immediately out of my nod. I had never heard him talk like that; a preacher saying a curse word.

At this point, three of the guys got right up and walked straight out of the house because they knew what was about to jump off was not good. One of the guys stayed, half nodding with his shoes off. My father took two steps toward me while I was still sitting in the chair and started to throw punches upside my head. I put my arms up like a boxer does in the ring to protect myself. I wasn't about to be foolish enough to even try to fight my father. The last guy in the room knew then, beyond a shadow of a doubt, that Bishop was for real. Out of the corner of my eye, I could see the last guy hopping out of the room trying to put on his shoes as he was leaving the room; for me that moment seemed like eternity.

My mother showed up at the door wringing her hands and crying, while my younger brother Tony was crying and hollering, "Daddy, don't kill him." I thought he was trying to kill me, too. I guess that was a sight. I realized that I had crossed the line and had pushed my father past his limit. After he was finished, he just grabbed me and hugged me and started crying. I was crying right along with him; crying because I had just received a painful, humiliating, royal butt whipping and realizing that I had hurt my father. My mother and Tony came into the room, and we all were hugging and crying together. My father and I never mentioned that incident for the rest of his life.

The fellas teased the messed out of me for the next few weeks, and I teased them about how fast they lost their high and got their behinds up out of there. I told the rest of them how Bruce was the last to leave, hopping out trying to put on his shoes while he was running out of the room. It wasn't funny to me then, but it's comical now when I think about how they booked up as we said in the streets when the blows started.

Chapter 7

(ABS)
"Always Be Strapped"

Before the term Anti-lock Breaking System, a few of us used the acronym ABS for "always be strapped," meaning always carry a gun. This was a necessity when selling drugs or being involved in a lot of shady dealings and/or being involved in both. As for carrying a gun for stick-ups and robbery, I learned early that armed robbery was not for me.

The first time I attempted to do a stick up, it turned out to be a farce. My father was an avid hunter, so he always had rifles and pistols. I knew where my father kept a pistol; a .25 cal. automatic. I took it one morning in the fall of 1968 after he had gone to work. I drove downtown in my Thunderbird. When you have a gun and are committing a robbery, you are the one in complete control of the situation, or so I thought. The mere presence of a gun stuck in someone's side, gut, back of the head or face does something to that person. It can make the meanest people become humble and willing to be obedient to your every command. It gives the person holding the gun a sense of power knowing they can take whatever a person has including their life.

This particular morning, I realized that at the age of

16, I didn't have what it took to end a life. At least not at that time. Although, a couple of years later the nerve and hardness of heart eventually came.

I parked around the corner and hid in a storefront on Griswold. As a man approached, I stepped out of the shadows and stood in front of him and showed the gun and announced a stick up. I thought it would go down like in the movies. You know, he would beg me not to shoot him and hand over all of his money and valuables; it didn't go like that at all. As a matter of fact he looked at the gun, and then he looked hard into my young face and did the strangest thing. He laughed. I often wondered what he saw that made him laugh. Was it this kid that he felt he could have easily overpowered, was he strapped with a gun himself and just as easily could have killed me? Or was it God just watching over my foolish behind once again?

Nowadays, there are kids that shoot and kill people for the slightest disrespect. After this incident, I realized that stickups were not my calling. If I was to ever pull a gun out again it would be only to separate a person, not just from their things but from this life, or to protect my own.

I did manage to pull off one stickup of a business, it was a clothing store on Woodward and Pasadena, called Park's Menswear. This was an inside job where I knew someone that worked in the store. His role was to make sure that no one did anything stupid. I was a year older than he was and I told him I was prepared to shoot. A guy named John went along with me on the stickup. We entered the store and John immediately herded the workers into a back room and had our inside person tie the others up. John tied him up last. While this was going on, I was in the front emptying out the cash register and loading up bags with accessories and clothes.

We forgot one small but very important thing, to lock the door. Wouldn't you know it? A customer walked in the store and mistook me for a salesperson. I told you robbery wasn't my thing. I should have just put the gun in his face and ushered him to the back with everybody else, instead I waited on him. He finally picked out a jacket and asked me the price. I made up a price off the top of my head. He went on to tell me that wasn't the price on the tag. It was so funny afterwards; it could have been an episode on the Martin Lawrence show or Sanford and Son where Fred would look at his son Lamont and say "You big dummy". I told him we were about to take inventory, so I would let him have it at 20% off. I made the sell. When we went to the cash register, I rung him up and gave him the total. Then, I remembered that I had all the money in my pockets. I was about to take him in the back room and have him tied up as well, but he had the exact change. I hurried him out of the store, locked the door and put up the "Closed" sign. We left out of the back door.

I was still in high school, yet I was a criminal who would rob, steal, cheat, con, eventually sell drugs, fence stolen goods, cash stolen checks, pimp, have boosters (a person that stole clothes) and then some. Crime was my stock and trade where I felt I could always get a dollar. Out of them all, armed robbery was the most senseless to me. I had to take many chances for too little money and to spend too much time in jail if and when I was caught. I figured if I wasn't going to rob banks or armored cars, then forget it. I still carried a gun nonetheless for my own protection.

This motto of ours Always Be Strapped, (ABS) came in handy while I was attending high school. That's why when I hear people talk about youth with guns today in school; I'm not surprised because I carried one myself from time to time while I was in high school. I had it in my locker or briefcase. I enjoyed the image I portrayed by carrying a briefcase in school I always thought it was classy. Yet, people would have been shocked if they had only known what I was carrying inside my briefcase. Besides, I viewed myself even then as an administrator, entrepreneur and businessman; unfortunately, my dealings were mostly illegal at the time. A friend of mine, Rickey H., left school that morning and went over to a drug dealer's house in the Roosevelt and Buchanan area on the Westside. It was early in the morning, after having hung out all night, they let him in the house because he was cool with them and went back to bed. In actuality, he wasn't so cool with them. He stole some drugs from them while they were sleeping. He came back to the school and he shared the score with a few of us. We did all the dope.

There were at least 20 of us in Highland Park High School that were using Boy, another name we called heroin, we also called it scag, H and Blow. Rickey H. wanted to go back to the same house that evening and cop. Lanny and I asked him was he sure the guy he stole the dope from didn't know that he was the one that had taken it. He went on to say "Naw, there was no way that the guy knew he took the dope." He went on to explain, how his woman was knocked out and the dope was lying in the open on a tray next to the bed. Furthermore, there were other people in the house and any of them could have taken it. What Rickey H. didn't know was that the other people in the house ended up stealing all of the rest of the dope and they put the blame on Rickey H. since he was the only one that had left.

The fools we were, we went over there. It was an upstairs flat and we went in. The doorman and a couple more guys greeted Rickey H., as if everything was all right. He introduced me and Lanny to the guys in the joint, which is what we called a drug house. We were sitting there on the couch in the middle room when the guy whose joint it was walked in and Rickey H. introduced us to him. He kind of shrugged us off with a wave. He called Rickey H. into the kitchen along with some of the guys that worked in the joint. They began talking to him and shut the door. We heard some scuffling, and then all of a sudden it was quiet. Lanny and I kept looking at each other, wondering what was going on.

Eventually, the guys came out and the head man proceeded to pick up the phone and call someone. We could tell by the way the conversation was going that he was calling somebody to take Rickey H. out. We found out that Rickey H. was in the kitchen tied up. They had tied him to a chair in the kitchen. It seemed as if someone else had gotten the same idea that Rickey H. had and took some dope while the people were asleep, but all the blame fell on him. He was about to pay the ultimate price for that indiscretion, his life. As I said, it probably was some of the guys that worked the dope joint. Lanny and I looked at each other and we were wondering, how we were going to get out of there and get Rickey H. out of there at the same time. Lanny and I were strapped; we had our pistols on us. We just waited.

We had come to the conclusion that if they were going to take Rickey H. out, they were going to take us out as well. Perhaps, they would have told us that we could leave or that this situation was none of our concern, but we weren't crazy. We figured that we weren't getting out alive. They eventually came into the room where we were sitting, sat down and started to watch us. They left Rickey H. in the kitchen. After awhile, we began to hear commotion in the kitchen. They ran to the kitchen only to find that Rickey H. had gotten up with the chair still tied to him and jumped out of the window from the second story. They were hollering, "Ah, man, he done jumped out the window." That was the clue for Lanny and I to bust up out of there, too. We looked at each other, pulled our pistols out and told them, "Don't nobody move." We walked back-to-back right out the place. When we reached outside, we ran to the car and rode around the neighborhood a couple of times, hollering for Rickey H. We thought that if he heard us and he was hiding in a yard somewhere he would run out and get in the car. We saw some of the guys from the house riding around, too. We figured that they also were looking for Rickey H. It was time for us to book up (leave quickly) out of there.

All we wanted to do was retaliate. We drove to Pontiac, Michigan, which is about 20 miles north of Detroit and picked up Bruce, who lived with his father. Bruce had artillery as well. We picked up Posse, who was about 350 pounds and looked liked an entire posse by himself. He was an excellent get-a-way driver for the ride back to the spot that Rickey H. had jumped from. Lanny and I explained the situation and who was in the house and where. At the time, we didn't believe in endangering children or older people; we had our limits. Nowadays, they will shoot in houses with babies and grandparents and anybody else, whether they are in the game or not. We didn't play that. We had some standards, however twisted they were, we lived and died by them.

We went back to the spot and shot the place up, through the walls, doors and windows; anywhere and everywhere. Afterwards, we rode around the block, knowing that they would come running out of the house to get into their cars to come after us or to get away. As we were turning the corner we could see them coming out. Posse gunned the engine in the car as we rode by letting out another barrage of gunfire on everybody standing, running or walking. After that, we never had a problem from them. All firearms were immediately discarded, never to be seen or used again. We didn't see Rickey H. for two days. He was a little bruised but all things considered, he was still alive.

Rickey H. eventually used his smile and charm, along with his gift of gab to become a player; he was pimping all over the country. He would breeze into town to visit with his family. We would get together and hang out during those visits. As of today, he is in prison doing a long sentence for dealing drugs.

For many years, we attributed our getting out of that situation to our street smarts or finesse, or whatever you want to call it. Of course, I didn't know it at the time but, when I look retrospectively at the entire situation, I now know that it was nothing but the grace of God.

They could have killed us when we first walked in the door, or even when we were sitting on the couch with our pistols at our waist. Think about it, they could have ushered the three of us into a room or taken us outside and shot us; anything could have happened. It was nothing but the grace of God in that entire situation.

Chapter 8

Jamaica

For the senior trip, our class chose to go to Jamaica. The previous graduating classes would go to Washington D.C., as a matter of tradition. We wanted to break tradition. I think the class before us actually broke the tradition, but we established it. Now, it is common practice for senior classes to go to the Caribbean or Mexico.

As class president along with the other officers, we formed a committee that was responsible for fund-raising events to help defray the cost. I can honestly say that high school was very enjoyable for me. I learned to fine tune my people skills, as well as learn to start using some of my administrative abilities. We planned, organized and made sure the trip was a successful, memorable and fun-filled event. It was definitely a highlight of the senior year of high school. We visited beaches, walked the waterfalls, and enjoyed a vacation that we never wanted to end.

When it was time for the trip, the group of us that had drug habits were worried about getting our drugs through customs. Posse, Bruce, Rufus and I had to take a week's supply with us. We didn't want to take the chance of trying to find a connection down there. We managed to get the drugs into Jamaica without getting busted.

While in Jamaica, we were turned on to some of the most potent weed (marijuana) that we had ever smoked. One of the hotel employees turned us on. Our little group made a side excursion one night to buy us a little weed while the rest of the group was having dinner. We only wanted a little, since it was so strong. We gave the Jamaican $5.00 U.S. and waited for him to come back. We were looking for him to come back with one of our regular nickel bags ($5). To our amazement and delight, what he came back with blew our minds. He had the weed rolled up in some newspaper shaped like a tube; about a foot long and two to three inches in diameter. It was worth over $100.00 back in Detroit. We smoked the rest of the trip and we bought some more to take home with us.

I told the other fellas to pace their use of heroin while in Jamaica. I explained that they needed it to last the whole trip, so that they wouldn't get sick before the trip was over. I only used what was necessary each day so that I wouldn't run out. A couple of them weren't as wise; they used theirs up in only a couple of days. I knew then that I had to hide my stash. We had two adjoining rooms. Rufus and I were in a room, while Posse and Bruce were in the other room. I found the perfect place to hide my stash. I hid it in **THEIR** room. Sure enough, when the trip was winding down to the last couple of days, they needed a fix.

I still had some of my drugs left. I only used in the mornings to get me through the day. One afternoon, I had gone to visit the room of some of the girls that had come on the trip. When I returned to my room it was in shambles, they had ransacked it looking for my stash. It never occurred to them to look in their own room for my drugs. I cursed them out and told them that mine was gone, too. I said I was just toughing it out and they had to do the same.

The game I played was this: acting as if I was real sleepy in the mornings, so I would be the last one to get out of bed they would go eat breakfast. While they were gone I would slip into their room, get my stash and get high, then go to breakfast. They knew I had some drugs, but I didn't care. I had to look out for my own habit.

On the morning that we were to leave for home, I showed them where I had my drugs stashed in their room. I shared what I had left with them because I had an ulterior motive. I wanted them to be mellow and not edgy, because we had to get the weed we purchased while we were in Jamaica back into the United States. I could not afford to have them sick and panicky. We made it through customs and the senior class trip to Jamaica was a success.

I left Jamaica involved in all kinds of foolishness, not knowing that years later I would be coming down regularly for vacations and leading missions trips as a Pastor, to Montego Bay, Ocho Rios and Mandeville.

Chapter 9

Oakland University

I graduated from Highland Park High School in June of 1970. I had been accepted to attend college at Oakland University in Rochester, Michigan. I started classes that summer. My parents took me to school and settled me in the Vandenberg Hall dormitory on campus.

My roommate was from Martin Luther King High School in Detroit, his name was Reginald Fields. He played the bass. He became a well known jazz bassist in the Detroit area and played in Europe, New York and nationally. He could always be found "scatting" in the room and on campus, so we gave him the nickname "Shoo Be Doo." It stuck with him and later became his trademark name in jazz circles. "Shoo Be Doo" and I maintained a friendship that lasted beyond college until his death twenty years later, around 1991.

I was settled on campus but there was a problem, my heroin habit. My parents dropped me off on Sunday, but I was back in Detroit before the week was out copping some dope. My parents knew that I had a drug problem. My mother took me to see our family physician to see what could be done to help. He prescribed medication to take with me to school.   The problem with prescribed medication was that it kept me drowsy or knocked out. It was worse than the heroin. I was unable to function and that was one of the drawbacks that illegal or legal drugs have.   If you were too high, it can stop your ability to function and reason properly.

I was taking classes and getting high, maintaining that double lifestyle. Going to college and being in a different environment didn't change the fact that I was still a drug addict and a criminal. I eventually came to realize that recovery doesn't come with a change of environment, but a change of attitude and behavior. My behavior was still the same. I began to look for ways to support my habit while I was there. I started doing what came natural, stealing tape decks from the cars in the parking lots. It was easier here than in the city of Detroit. The problem was that I didn't have a car to drive to the city to fence my stuff. I would load them in a briefcase or small suitcase and hitchhike to the city. Sometimes I would visit my parents, other times I would sell my stolen goods, cop some drugs and pay one of my friends to take me back to school. Hitchhiking was very simple at that time and people weren't reluctant to give a nice looking, mannerable student a ride.

I broke into a storage room in the dormitory and found the belongings of a student that was gone home for the summer. He lived in Bloomfield Hills, Michigan, which is known as a very affluent suburban area. He had left his checkbook, as well. I thought to myself, "Well, I'll be." I knew I had one month to get busy cashing checks. The first thing I did was to get a temporary student I.D. and a couple of preppy looking outfits to wear so that I could look as though I lived in Bloomfield Hills. I took on the personhood of Ellsworth Anderson III and went on a spree. I didn't try to cash any of the checks off of campus because there was a sweet set up in the school system for me to take advantage of.

I simply would go into the bookstore on campus with a list of books for certain classes and purchase the textbooks. The most expensive books were on my list. Some I would locate in the store on my own or sometimes I would solicit the help of one of the staff persons on the pretext that I was unable to locate a particular book. They would be helpful and I would engage them in conversation to the point where they became comfortable with me. This was done so that when I came back, in their mind, I was someone that they knew. I learned that while carrying out the confidence game, that real con is executed with such precision and planning that the targeted marks didn't have a clue that they are being manipulated to act in my best interest. The con, when done with such finesse will have the mark, which was the person being played, think that it was their idea or for their own benefit.

After purchasing the books with the stolen checks and the fake student I.D., I would take them to the refund counter the next day with the receipt and get cash money back. I would tell the clerk that I was dropping the class, switching classes or changing my major, if they would ask.

I did this during different shifts, with different staff people working the cash registers and refund counters. It was a very lucrative month. I was able to save money for later use. Saving money to get high later just makes sense to an heroin addict. When I started using crack cocaine, like so many others, I wasn't able to save a dime. The difference was that I could only do so much heroin or I would overdose. I could never shoot $200.00 worth of heroin at one time, whereas with cocaine, I would be able to smoke thousands of dollars before getting up from the table a few days later. This made sense to me and to all people that smoked cocaine. "Smoke 'til all the money is gone," that was the "addictive thinking" of addiction. Whereby one would look to justify and make sense of all behavior that was really insensible.

At the start of the third quarter while at Oakland University, I discovered some students who were selling big time weed on campus. They lived in the same dormitory, only in the other wing. I told a friend from Detroit, Dwight Holman, about their drug dealing and set up. He agreed to help me rob them. In order to gain entrance into the dormitory, we had to sign in at the front desk in the evening. We signed in, went to my room to get high until it was time to commit the robbery. Instead of going back past the front desk to get to the other wing, we slipped out of the back door of my wing. I jimmied the lock and we were in the other wing. It was about 3:00 a.m. We knocked on the door and gave the code name. One of the guys opened the door. He immediately found a pistol in his face and was instructed to turn around so that he could not to see our faces. There were three of them in the room, and we had them turn around and face the wall so that they could not see our faces. Dwight tied them up while I held the gun on them. I trusted myself to be calm yet handle any situation that may have came up without hesitation. That is why I held the gun. After tying them up, Dwight put made them all fall into the same bed and put the cover over them.

In Detroit a drug dealer would have come to the door with a pistol or shotgun in his hand, or one person would have opened the door and another person would have been strapped behind the door. We didn't have any resistance, only the pleas not to shoot them. We took all their money and then loaded a suitcase with the marijuana. We left them there, tied up and left out the back door into the car that we had and headed back to Detroit. The next day, we had no trouble at all unloading the high-grade weed. I was back at school the next evening.

I heard it through the grapevine that the boys had reported the robbery. Naturally, they didn't tell the police anything about drugs being stolen. They claimed that they were only robbed of some money, stereo equipment and jewelry.

Warrants were issued for our arrest for armed robbery. The police were basing this solely on the fact that we signed in that night and had previous records. Very weak evidence, but people have been convicted with less initial evidence. We eventually were charged with armed robbery in Oakland County. Dwight was arrested in Highland Park and transferred to Oakland County. When he was released on bond, he found me and told me everything. We rehearsed the story that we stayed in my dorm room until the next morning and then went to Detroit; we knew nothing about an armed robbery. A week after he was arrested and arraigned, the detectives called my house and talked to my father and told him that I was wanted for questioning.

At the time, I was already on probation for UDAA, unlawfully driving away an automobile. My father was not about to have the police come to his house looking for me. As he told me before, "You do not bring any reproach on my house." Remember, he had already physically beat me down once for having stolen goods in his house. He was not having it. He told me that I had two choices, leave his house or ride with him to Pontiac, Michigan, which had jurisdiction of the case, to turn myself in. I told him that I didn't do it and that they couldn't possibly have a case against me. He said, "In that case you don't have anything to worry about," and off to the Pontiac police station he took me. I couldn't believe it, but I didn't have anywhere else to go and I wasn't about to live on the streets hiding out. I felt the case against us was circumstantial, at best.

Bishop took me to the jail, gave me the detective's name and drove off. I couldn't believe it, he didn't even bother to wait and see what was going to happen to me. I didn't know it at the time, but he had his ways and means of keeping tabs on me. I was tempted to call my friend Bruce, who lived in Pontiac to come and get me. I decided to get it over with. I waited until the detective came out. He arrested me on the spot and took me straight up to Clarkston, Michigan for arraignment before a judge. The judge asked me how I pleaded and I told him not guilty. I told him "Your Honor, I am a student and I am interested in becoming a lawyer. For me to commit a crime, especially one of this magnitude would be insane. I would never be able to practice law locked up or with a felony conviction or being a career criminal" I pleaded with the Court to dismiss the case that had so frivolously been brought against me." The judge told me that he was letting the charge stand, but he would release me on my own recognizance to come back with legal representation.

After the hearing, I was escorted back to Oakland County Jail. I called my father to pick me up, which he did. No matter what, my father was very supportive of me. He obtained a lawyer for me. In fact, not just any lawyer. He called a well-known criminal attorney that attended Northwestern High School with him, Cornelius Pitts; however, We could not afford him at the time. Mr. Pitts told my father of his exorbitant fee and suggested that we contact a very brilliant young attorney in Pontiac, Michigan that was making a name for him self; the attorney was Elbert Hatchett of the law firm Hatchett, Brown, Waterman and Campbell. His retainer fee and daily court appearance fee then was much less than Cornelius Pitts'.

We were in court twice and the case was dismissed. I was informed that under no uncertain terms by the head of Campus Security at Oakland University, I could not apply for admittance in the upcoming quarter; that was fine by me. I decided to attend classes at Wayne State University.

Dwight was eventually shot in the back after attempting to rob an associate of his. Dwight's associate was in possession of a sizable amount of money and was treating Dwight and Bo real good by letting them get high with him. The guy was paying Michael (a.k.a. Fish) to drive them around. After getting high, Dwight told Fish to turn into an alley so that he could use the restroom. When they got in the alley, Dwayne and Bo pulled a gun out on the guy and attempted to rob him. I guess they thought that they could easily rob the guy. They were wrestling for the pistol in the car and the guy ended up with it. Dwight and Bo took off running down the alley. While they were running down the alley, a shot hit Dwight in the back and paralyzed him from the waist down and the next shot took off a piece of Bo's nose. Dwight died later from complications of the paralysis after spending several years in a wheel chair.

Chapter 10

The Shooting Gallery

Before Lanny learned how to shoot himself with heroin, I had to hit him. On one occasion, while doing this in my house, my father caught us. Bishop read us the riot act and asked us why were we willing to throw our lives away, when we had so much going for us. He sent Lanny home. Lanny didn't come to visit for almost a year.

I had shot drugs before in dope houses where I copped. A few friends and I would sit around a table and shoot up our drugs. We would talk about jazz, who we saw play and where. We would trade escapades, lies and fantasies while we were in the dope house. We would go to the shooting gallery and shoot drugs in our arms. If anyone was shooting up anywhere else, it was in private, in the bathroom or in the bedrooms in the back.

No one can prepare you psychologically for what you would see, the first time you enter a shooting gallery, which is a place where addicts go to shoot up, using their drugs intravenously; without interruption. It was a place away from home, where I wouldn't have to worry about family members walking in and busting me.

This particular day, we were downtown and had copped on John R. and Erskine. We were sick. We hadn't had any drugs in a while. We couldn't wait and drive all the way back home to shoot up our drugs. One of us asked, "Hey Shorty, where can we do our stuff at around here?" Shorty replied, "You can go over to Johnny's and do up, but you got to pay a couple of dollars." That was the standard fee to get into a shooting gallery, usually two dollars. If you had spent your last money to cop your dope, then you could offer the houseman a piece of your dope. Some people paid their rent and supplied their enormous drug habits by turning their apartments into shooting galleries.

Shorty took us to an apartment building on Erskine and up a couple of flights of dark, urine scented stairs. There was a naked light bulb that was on in front of the door. The purpose was to allow the doorman to see who wanted to come in. When we were approaching the door of the apartment, we could hear all sorts of conversation and hollering coming from inside. After Shorty knocked on the door, we waited with anticipation to get into a safe place to shoot up our heroin. We heard a lock being unlatched and the door cracked open a few inches. There was the face of a man that glared at the three of us, who looked as though he belonged in a horror picture. We could smell not only the stench of his alcohol breath and lack of bathing, but a rancid odor that would make the strongest stomach weak and throw up with one whiff.

"Who's that with you Shorty?" the doorman asked. "These some young bloods that copped some stuff and got to do up in a hurry." Shorty had already told us to give him our two dollars, which he held in his hand for the doorman to see. One thing I learned is that money has a certain effect on the greed of people. It will make someone drop their guard, allow anyone in their house and around their possessions. Addicts would subject themselves to all sort of danger for the love of money and getting high.

The doorman took the chain off the door and opened it wide to let us into the hell hole that I will never forget. The sight that greeted us a scene straight from the picture, Dantes Inferno or the novel Divine Revelation of Hell. There were people all over this apartment in every room. There weren't just a handful of dope fiends around a dining room or kitchen table that we had become accustomed to. There were people everywhere in the apartment; on the couch in the living room, the dining room, bathroom, all over, shooting up.

I learned later that the stench, I smelled in the hallway was coming from the open sores and abscesses running with puss and infection that people had on their bodies. When it is your first time in this kind of place it is difficult to keep your cool. You have to walk pass as if you're used to this kind of scene all the time. Yet, you're looking out of the corner of your eye and sometimes just outright staring at the scenes that are totally foreign to you. I didn't know that this would become a regular and comfortable place where I would get high on many occasions. If not this spot, someplace similar, in that there were shooting galleries all over the city.

We had to step over a girl lying on the living room floor. At first I thought she had OD'd or was dead. She had newspaper spread under her head so blood wouldn't run on the floor. There was a guy kneeling over her, shooting heroin into her neck. "Turn your head fool and quit trying to look at me b - - - -." "I got to look at your thieving a - - or you'll steal all my dope." I found out later that when you were getting someone to shoot you in your neck, it was best to know and trust who you had doing the job. Some people, while your head was turned would squirt some of your dope out into a cooker they stashed close by. You had to turn your head to the side so that they could see the juggler vein clearly in order to shoot the dope in it. This was a chance a person took with their life every time they had drugs shot in their neck. There are all types of horror stories where people's voice box and nerves were being damaged, because of drugs not being shot correctly into their necks. An abscess would form on the neck because the quinine that was used to cut the drugs had eaten through the tissue.

There was a guy and his whore in the bathroom. He was sitting on the toilet with his pants down around his ankles as she was shooting him up with heroin in his groin. Let me take a moment to clear up a certain point. Contrary to popular belief of those outside the drug culture, shooting up in the groin is not injecting the drugs into your penis or in the vagina. It is shooting into the iliac vein right at the fold of the thigh and hip area. After seeing this, I made the naive declaration as a novice dope user, before becoming an addict and fiend, that I would never shoot dope in my hands, neck, feet or groin. I lied. I eventually shot everywhere I could find a good vein.

Chapter 11

Nine – To – Five

My father didn't believe in a grown man lying around the house and not working. So, after I was forced to leave Oakland University, I had to find a job. I figured I couldn't hold a job and still try to hustle for drugs. I checked into my first methadone clinic at Herman Keifer Hospital on John C. Lodge to maintain some sense of normalcy in my life. Methadone is usually not to stop using heroin; it is simply a substitute, which allows an addict to maintain their ability to function without heroin. It allows a person to go to work, spend time with their family and start to get a life if the individual was really interested in real recovery. I remember when my counselor, Ms. Lloyd, took a great interest in me and tried to get me to go to Narcotics Anonymous, commonly known as NA meetings. I asked her if it was mandatory to attend in order for me to get my methadone. She said, "no," so I didn't go. It would be another 20 years, from 1971 through 1991, of using drugs and living a life of misery and degradation, before I realized that the program had something to offer me. Like they say in NA, "It's not for those that need it but for those that want it."

I was hired in the mailroom at J. Walter Thompson Advertising Company, which was located in the Buhl Building in Downtown Detroit. In the mailroom, we rotated our work schedules on Saturdays so that only one of us worked. We did this because the rest of the company was off and there wasn't a need for all of us to be there.

One particular Saturday it was my turn to work. When I was delivering mail, I noticed some checks in an office that was handling an advertising campaign. Well, I didn't actually just "notice" them. I was rifling through as many offices and desks that I could, whenever the opportunity presented itself. My criminal mind immediately went into overdrive. I took a handful of checks from the bottom of the box and went to the finance office. Once there, I used the facsimile signature and check writing machine with multiple colors and printed in various amounts on each check. I was set to start hanging paper -- cashing bogus checks.

I formed a crew to cash the checks that was complete with false identification. I would type in the names on the checks with an IBM Typewriter, and the crew would go to different stores and banks to cash the checks; while I went to work every day in the mailroom of the very company I had stolen the checks from as if nothing was amiss. We were staying in rooms in the Ponchartrain Hotel and the Sheraton Cadillac downtown. We had plenty of checks and with the proper identification, all we needed was a level head and plenty of nerve. One of the guys that was on the crew, Lonnie Mitchell, is now a born again Christian and a member of my church. God has done a miraculous work in his life. After experiencing addiction, jail, homelessness and pushing a grocery cart down the street with all of his belongings as a result of it, he is now a entrepreneur and landlord.

I learned from the experience with my grandmother's checks, that around the first of the month, a bank statement would be mailed to the check holder after about three weeks, so we would quit. I used some of the money from this escapade to finance my first start in what I call the "hard" drug business. I had sold a little weed to my friends in high school to support my own heroin habit, but this was different. I was ready to rock and roll.

Chapter 12

Dealer

I first started selling heroin in 1971 after I left Oakland University to support my drug habit. Me and a partner, Jerry, a.k.a. "Flu," would buy some wholesale weight- that was a nice quantity of drugs. We would package it as was and resell it for a profit. We had a built-in clientele from those we knew were users. We started selling it right from the basement of his mother's house on Waverly in Highland Park. Jerry's family had so many people coming in and out of their house and coming over to hangout that when we started selling the drug traffic wasn't really noticeable. I continued selling drugs off and on until I was sent to prison in 1980. Afterwards, I started back in 1985 until about 1990.

Lanny had quit using drugs. He had a job and was working for Ford Motor Company. He married his high school sweetheart and raised a family; later he and his wife divorced. He joined my father's church, Faith Tabernacle, and gave his life to the Lord. Lanny became an ordained minister and an associate pastor, and I was so proud of him. He would always ask me when I was going to quit using and my response would be, "One day."

There was a time when I wasn't selling drugs.

Bishop convinced me that I had skills in carpentry and that I should take some classes that were offered at Cass Technical High School in the evening for skilled trades. He explained to me that it was obvious that I didn't like working a normal "Nine to Five" job for other people, in a regular setting. He said that a man should use whatever skills and talents he has to make a living legitimately. He also explained that I wouldn't have to take chances stealing and going to jail, there were other ways to hustle and earn a clean living within the skilled trades. That was some of the best advice that he had given me. Bishop not only took me to enroll in school, he enrolled himself into the program as well. I realized later that it wasn't for his benefit but to walk with me and mentor me through to completion. I loved him for that. Years later, after I gave my life to Christ, I started my own construction company.

Whenever I wasn't selling drugs, the word was always on the street. Dealers would find out where I was, so that they could come to me to help them start a spot. They wanted to hire me to do the carpentry work to fortify the dope houses with solid core doors, reinforced with plywood. The doors would have doubled jambs, extra long screws, steel bars, peep holes and slots to pass the money and drugs through. I would build hide away stash places in various parts of the houses, such as closet floors, under stairways and behind the casings of windows.

There was an old user, we called "Kidd". and he was a master at mixing jive. He was the oldest of four brothers and a sister. The Hill brothers were from LaBelle Street , not related to the Bobby Joe Hill family, and "Kidd" was the first one to show me how to mix dope. There have been many a would-be dealers that started out with the best grade of heroin, only to mess it up because they didn't know how to cut and mix it properly.

When a dealer puts a cut on heroin it usually was done in one of two ways. The first way is to purchase it at a strong quality and put lactose or Manitol on it, and bag it up and sell it. This was usually for those that snorted it (inhaled through the nose) or for other dealers that would buy a quarter of an ounce or more. They would take the weight that they had bought and package it into red gelatin capsules, which we called "penny caps" and sell it. The second way is to make mix jive or scramble. Mix jive was for those that shot up their heroin. The heroin was mixed with lactose and quinine. A few years later when the quality of heroin lessened, dealers would add dormaine, a sleeping capsule to mix in to help cause the users to fall into a stupor.

In the early 70s a grade of heroin hit the streets called Mexican Mud. It was called this because of its dark brown color. If it wasn't kept cool and dry, it would get sticky and it would become hard to mix. Not much could be mixed at one time either, because the sugar in the lactose would weaken if it sat too long. To mix it, **we'd** bake the lactose in the oven until it was a light brown in color. Yet, if it stayed in the oven too long, it would turn gooey.

In the 1970s, sticking up dope houses and robbing dealers became a common thing. By the mid 70s dealers stopped letting customers come in to cop. They would have them pass the money and drugs through the slots in the doors or underneath the door. Around 1976, while I was selling drugs, there were a couple of guys, J.T. and Reggie that had the idea to stick me up. J.T. and I had a running feud but Reggie had grown up with my oldest brother, Mo, and I considered him a friend. It goes to show you drugs and money will change friends into enemies. They were hanging out at a gambling house, down the street from where my family and I lived on Ford Street, in Highland Park. At the time, I was married and had two children: Tamara, whom we called Micki and Ricardo Jr., whom we called Rick.

While they were at the gambling house hashing out their plan, a couple of guys overheard them talking, and they came down the alley to my back door and put me up on what J.T. and Reggie had in mind. I thanked them the way I knew how, by giving them each a couple packs of drugs. I got in my car and drove down the street and parked in front of the gambling house. I had an automatic pistol under a newspaper on the seat next to me. I waited for them to come to the car to make a move. I was ready to kill both of them in the street, knowing that they had a pistol and sawed-off shotgun. I figured I could beat the case with the justification of a minor gun charge. Somehow they must have known that I was ready because they never came off the porch and I drove away. This was the element I lived in and these were the kind of guys that I hung with. You always had to watch your back, it's a part of the game.

Later on that day, they stuck up another guy, "Bo Peep" and killed him. The word on the street spread and Reggie told my brother, Mo, that he never had any intentions of sticking me up. I told my brother to tell Reggie to stay out of the feud that was going on between J.T. and I. About a week after the murder, J.T. came by an apartment on Pingree and Second, where I was also staying with one of my ladies.

I decided not to buzz J.T. in and he started cussing in the intercom. Having a shootout on the street was one thing, but I wasn't going to allow him into my home and put the young lady that I was staying with in jeopardy or our son, Steven. The next thing we knew, gunshots were being fired at our apartment. Thank God we were on the top floor. Reggie came to my brother, Mo, and told him that he didn't have anything to do with it; that he just drove J.T.

over there and didn't have any idea that the guy would be shooting. I made a decision right then and there that he needed to be done.

I stalked Reggie for a few days. He would get up in the morning and walk his grandmother's dog around Thompson and the Davison/Lodge Expressway before he would start his day. On the day that I was driving by about to do my business, God intervened. I didn't recognize it as Him at the time, though. I wasn't going to do a drive by and have my car spotted. I didn't want anyone else involved because in my mind this was personal, not business. Besides, I needed information on J.T.'s whereabouts as well.

My plan was to get him into the car under the pretense that we were going to get high and bury whatever misunderstandings we had and all would be forgiven. I had the joint I wanted picked out. I rode up on him as he was walking down the street and told him to come and ride with me. As he was getting into the car, police cars came from everywhere. They surrounded us with pistols drawn and demanded that we get out the car with our hands in view. People started looking out of their windows and coming on their porches in seconds. The thought crossed my mind that it was a good thing I didn't do a drive by. Thinking back now, the neighbors would have had a description of my car and possibly me as well or, the police would have witnessed it and I would have had an iron clad murder one case, without a chance of beating it.

I hollered to the police that I had a pistol in my waistband and that I didn't want to get shot. I did this so that the people on their porches could hear me as I was getting out of the car from the driver's seat. An elderly woman shouted back, "You telling 'em right, son." I was relieved that I was not going to be a statistic in the morgue that day.

As it turned out, the police were looking for J.T. and Reggie for the "Bo Peep" killing. On this particular morning when they found Reggie and saw me, they mistook me for J.T. and thought they had their two suspects. When we arrived at the Highland Park jail, Reggie asked me if I was planning on taking him out with the pistol I had. I told him I only wanted to talk to him.

Once we went to court, I ended up with a charge for CCW, Carrying a Concealed Weapon. Reggie was charged with murder in the first degree. He told the court that J.T. was not involved in the killing. Reggie is still serving time now 33 years later. He is the Chairman of the National Lifers of America. My brother, Mo, still writes and visits him from time to time. No one has heard from J.T., we figured he must have left town. Reggie wrote me a later recently and stated that he never meant me any harm and didn't realize how volatile the relationship was between me and J.T. Drugs will cloud your mind and your memory.

Prior to my actual court date, I decided to skip town and went to Los Angeles to live with another uncle and aunt, Ronnie and Diane. The court issued a fugitive warrant for my arrest because I missed the court date. I ended up hanging with a friend of mine, Clyde, who was the person I first started shooting dope with. He won a settlement and after the settlement he had a nice sum of money. We went to Los Angeles together to establish a connection to start our own pipeline of drugs into Detroit.

During the time while I was in Los Angeles, I learned about "free basing" cocaine. This was the new method on the West Coast for getting high. Mixing the cocaine with ether would remove all the impurities. The residue left behind would be scraped up with a razor blade and smoked. This process is actually very dangerous because the ether used in the process is flammable. Years later, using baking soda and heating it up in a vial became an easier way to process it. A rock would form and this is what was smoked. At the time, I thought it was such a waste of dope. I felt the best way to do drugs without all the foolishness, was to just shoot it straight into the vein and get it immediately into the system. Little did I know that six years later I would be smoking cocaine. Eventually, we made our connection through some friends and my uncle Ray, who moved to Los Angeles, also.

Clyde went back to Detroit to sell the heroin and was to contact me when he was finished. Two weeks had passed and I hadn't heard anything from him. The dope that I had for myself, from my very first transaction was running low. I wasn't in Los Angeles a month and I had used up all the dope; I was sick. I had to call Bishop and ask him to send me plane fare to come back home. Thank God for a father that loved me in spite of my foolishness. I would learn years later that God was just like that too.

Once I had gotten back to Detroit, the first thing I did was cop some dope to get straight. I had been sick for a couple of days and I wasn't even trying to quit at this time. I found Clyde; he had been playing Mr. Big Shot and blew all his money. As the old saying goes, "a fool and his money will soon part." I couldn't get mad at him. After all, it was his money. My only regret was that I didn't stay with him to get what I could get, but going to California was a way for me to dodge my case.

Now, here I was, back in Detroit with a fugitive warrant out for me. I eventually ended up getting stopped on a traffic violation and the warrant came up. I had to post bond and get a new court date. I had a scheduled court date in Wayne County Circuit Court before Judge Sullivan. My case couldn't be found; they said they would contact me about a future court date which never came. To God be the glory, because I didn't pay anyone and I didn't have a high priced lawyer or anything.

Faith Tabernacle had already moved once in 1969 from the storefront building. The church purchased a building of storefronts which had apartments upstairs. The walls were knocked down so that it would be one large sanctuary. The rooms were used as offices and classrooms. When I returned from California, Faith Tabernacle was in the process of moving to its third location, which was a large building on Hamilton Avenue. Hamilton Avenue is a large thoroughfare in the city of Highland Park and the Detroit Metropolitan area. The building was bought from a catering company. I remember walking through the building before it was remodeled and I found payroll checks that the catering company had left behind. The name on the checks was Roummell Catering, which was a well known company in the Detroit metropolitan area. They were famous for catering all of the Cobo Hall events at the time and cashing their checks would be easy. Needless to say, once again I was off and running. I recruited a stable of women to cash the checks; Carol, Rita, and JoAnn were all down; they had been cashing checks for awhile. They had different identification and disguises to go along with them. During these days, the stores didn't have all the sophistication that they have now such as Comp-U-Check or TeleCheck to see if the checks were stolen or the accounts were inactive.

I would pick the ladies up in a van and drive them to different banks and liquor stores that cashed checks, and the ladies would cash about three checks a piece each time we went out. We kept a record of what stores were hit and when, so we would know approximately when they would receive the bad checks back and we wouldn't go there again. We would split the money 60/40, since I had the paper (checks), typewriter and check writer; 60 percent to me and 40 to them. We were one big happy family.

In 1977, I started helping a friend of mine Robert Barnes "Barnes". work his joint, which is the common term for a dope house or spot, as they call it in today's terms. The joint was located in an area known as the North End of Detroit. This joint was on Oakland and Philadelphia above a laundromat. It had been previously used as an after-hour spot. The spot was opened from about 2:00 in the afternoon until 10:00 p.m. at night. Eventually, "Barnes" was sent to jail on another case. Our friends Dave, Mike, and Rob that we were copping from asked me if I wanted to take the joint over. Of course, this was an opportunity that I wasn't about to turn down. The joint was already established and had a thriving clientele. I kept the joint open 24/7; 24-hours a day, seven days a week. We didn't close on Sundays or holidays because addicts get high and need drugs each and everyday. In 1978, I opened another spot on the West side in an apartment building on Taylor at

Linwood. There was a guy, Terry, who lived in the neighborhood where I grew up, and he ran the joint for me.

By this time, the veins in my arms had all collapsed, they had sunk so far into the tissue from shooting drugs over the years. I started shooting in my hands; something I said I would never do. I was shooting dope in the morning when I got up, around noon, in the late afternoon or early evening and before I went to bed. I had what is known as a dealer's habit. My hands would swell sometimes from not shooting directly into the vein. I would put on an ace bandage and tell the non-users that I slammed my hand in a car door or something. I remember once when my father asked me, "Rick, how many times does it take you to get your hands out the way? You slammed the other one last month." I knew that he knew what time it was. I had sunk another step lower and started shooting in my legs and feet; places I said I would never, ever go. After that, I learned I would never say never, or what I would not do as long as I was shooting heroin.

I begun having trouble getting a hit and someone told me about a lady, Sandra who was good at hitting people. We called these people "doctors," so someone took me to meet her. The next thing I remember, I was laying on the floor, like the scenes I had viewed in the shooting galleries of people laying on the floor, taking a deep breath and having someone shoot dope in the vein of their neck. I would give Sandra a "blow", a pack of dope each time she hit me. I could afford it, after all, I had the sack. Her habit, of course, increased as well, to say the least. Sometimes she would sell the pack to have extra money. I came up with the idea to have her work one of the shifts in the spot on Oakland Avenue. I felt it was a win/win situation. She worked and got a salary, plus dope and I received her services for free.

When a person works a spot, they would get what was commonly known in the drug trade as "the tops." The pack of heroin that would sell for $12, ten dollars would go to the dealer and the two dollars, which was the "tops," would go to the runners or the person working the joint. If a person sold a hundred packs that day that was $200.00 in their pocket. I would give the people working for me the "tops," and two packs of dope. Frequently, workers would attempt to steal out of the bags or try to place their own product in with the dealers, and the dealers knew this. The workers also knew, if caught, there would be dire consequences to be paid.

The spot on Oakland was busted one day. Sandra was working her shift and went to jail. I couldn't get her out on bond because she had a previous warrant out for her arrest. I had to shoot the dope myself, again. This was so frustrating because I couldn't find a vein. Even to this day, when I go for a physical, the lab technicians have a difficult time finding a vein to draw blood; they have to stick me several times. I leave with band-aids all over my arms and hands.

I was driving and spotted another "doctor," Carl, and I got him to hit me. Carl showed me how to use the one-inch long needle for shooting myself in the groin. In the drug life of heroin addicts it wasn't strange at all to see a guy having another guy help get a hit in the groin. This was no homosexual activity; it was just the norm in our world. The only thing that was on our mind was getting the dope in a vein to get high. I never had to worry about a hit after that. I would go from one side to the other in order to let the other rest. Eventually, I had no other choice but to use the 1 ½ long needles.

In 1978, I was arrested for a sales and delivery of drug charge at the Taylor Street drug house I had. This was such a trumped up charge. I happened to drive up as the police were coming up the street to raid the joint. Terry was up in the joint but I was in my car, clean with no drugs on me, just coming to pick up my money. The police spotted me and snatched me out of the car and took me up with them while they kicked in the door to my joint and then threw me inside and said I was in the joint. Terry and I were released on bond. I wasn't out a month when I caught another case. The courts combined both charges together. I took a cop, which is commonly known in the legal system as a plea bargain to a possession charge, and I received two years probation. Judge Kerwin told me that if I violated this probation and came back before him, that he would not hesitate to send me to prison. I knew that if the police got word that I was still dealing, they wouldn't waste any time locking me up. I backed away from the hustle. However, I still had a habit to take care of. I got into a methadone program to bring my habit under control. I started putting my carpentry skills to work by remodeling houses, although, I would still hustle the streets in between jobs.

Chapter 13

Trying To Quit

There were many times that I tried to quit using and stay off drugs. I would try on my own power, by making many resolutions and promises to myself, parents, my wife at the time, and to God. In reality, they were nothing more than confessions because I didn't change; the promises were not enough. The commitment and lack of conviction just weren't there. I wasn't strong enough to stay off alone, because I never changed my attitude and behavior in any way. I had been in so many methadone clinics that I lost count. While in the methadone clinics, I would get some sort of relief. I would get relief from not only shooting up heroin, which was damaging my body, but also relief from hustling, scheming, and taking chances on going to jail or getting killed in order to get up on the money to buy drugs. There would be times when I would do both, take the methadone and still use heroin. It was a hellish existence.

I remember when my first daughter, Tamara, was born in 1975. I cried like a baby, because she was going to have a junkie for a father. I was determined to really stop using. No way was my daughter going to grow up knowing I used dope. I think I quit for about a week. Then when my second child Rick Jr., was born, a year later in 1976, I really, really meant it then. Needless to say, it was with the same results. I hear so many people say, "They (addicts) don't want nothing, they don't want to quit using, and all they have to do is stop." What people fail to realize is that some drug addicts do want to quit, they just don't know how. There is no realization that you have a choice. Often people who are addicted feel as though they don't have a choice; their only means of existence is to use drugs or whatever their addiction may be.

You are caught in the grips of a force that is stronger than yourself. The thing that grows the strongest in your life is the thing that is fed the most. The thing that is starved will die. I was feeding and living a life of drugs and sin. Drug use becomes a life dominating sin that affects every area of your life. I couldn't get a job because I couldn't pass a physical. If fortunate enough to have a job, it is difficult to keep because getting high will come first. As a result, the job is lost. If you are in school, you begin to neglect your studies and homework just to feed your craving for drugs. Your grades drop and before you know it, you're skipping classes and going over friend's houses, whose parents aren't at home to get high and have unprotected sex. Whatever social activities you are involved in soon are centered on getting drugs. Eventually, all recreational activities cease because all your time is consumed in getting high or trying to get the money to get high. Your family becomes less important to you. This is a reality that many people do not want to admit. You will hear or make comments like, "Oh no, my wife and kids come before anything", "I wouldn't do anything to bring shame to my parents," "I love my family". The longer you use drugs, there is no way that the drugs will not take priority over your family. You will miss your children's recitals, anniversaries, birthdays, holidays, weddings, funerals and other special events.

When you get in trouble, you begin to make promises to God that you will never keep. "Oh God if you just get me out of this, I promise I'll change," or "I'll never do this again," or "God, just let me get this money this last time and I'll quit for real".

A couple of years later in 1978, when Morris, with my wife at the time, and Steven, with a different woman were born, I wasn't even trying to quit. As a matter of fact, I was on a roll selling dope and I was content. I wasn't trying to hide my lifestyle from anyone. I was married and had a lady on the side, and a drug habit that I could afford to take care of. I was so desensitized to other's feelings that I had the attitude that if you didn't like it, lump it. If I felt myself feeling or getting emotional, I would do what I did best, anesthetize it with drugs.

I was on a roller coaster that I was unable to get off of. I had become so accustomed to this lifestyle that I really began to think that the only escape would be death. Yet, I still had no desire to die in this lifestyle. I just knew that I would not live to be 35 or 40 years old. I was plagued with all types of nightmares of dying as a result of my lifestyle. Dying from an overdose, getting shot by some body trying to rob me or being taken out execution style with a bullet in my brain. I would dream about lying in the casket and no one came to the funeral. Then there was the one where people would come just to see if I was really dead and then they were glad about me no longer being on this earth.

The only thing close to a break would come when I went to prison. I say, "close to a break" because I still continued to live a hustler's life while I was locked up.

Chapter 14

INMATE # 162974

I had about six more months before I would be off probation. I received a phone call from my friends Dave, Mike and Rob saying they were back in the box, dealing drugs again. They asked if I was ready to rock and roll. I wanted in on the action. The lure of the easy money and call of the wild street life was tempting. The Bible says, "Blessed is the man that endures temptation and doesn't give in to it," I guess I wasn't really blessed then, because I only looked at temptation as an opportunity to have pleasure or to make money. Later on I came to realize that temptation is really an opportunity to show God how much you love Him more than something or some one else. Needless to say I yielded.

Things were back to normal. They supplied the

drugs up front, and I ran the crew. I wasn't out of any pocket expenses. I had about four people working at the time. We took it to one of the places of fast action; we went to Downtown Detroit by the Brewster Projects. Selling drugs had come out from behind apartment doors and houses and onto the streets. Dealers began selling their product right on the corners, from hidden stashes, that would be located under rocks, behind garbage cans and in vacant houses or buildings. Dealers had the "runners" selling the dope like they were hawking refreshments at a basketball or football game. You could ride down the street and hear the various names the dealers gave their product or dope to identify it. "Hoochi Con, Top Ten, Murder One, Smiling Faces, A-1," was being yelled by the dealers. We also gave a name that fitted the circus environment where we were selling. We called it "Red Hots." You could hear the runners hollering, "Get your Red Hots, Get Your Red Hots here." The traffic was so thick in that area and the surrounding streets in the projects on Brush, John R, Erskine, Alfred, and St. Antoine.

I gave my crew ten bundles at a time; a bundle was 12 packs. Each pack sold on the street for $12. Two packs out of the twelve and the "tops" which was $2, went to the runner so they could clear $40 a bundle. They turned in $100 to me for each bundle. I gave my supplier $60 a bundle and I would clear $40 per bundle. For every 10 bundles I would profit $400. All I had to do was distribute.

It was a good run that ended abruptly for me. One morning I drove down to our area, on Alfred between John R. and Brush, to meet my crew and give them their bundles. After I distributed the dope, I went in the store on the corner and bought a Detroit Free Press Newspaper. I read the paper daily. I was glancing at the paper while I was in line and heard the cries from the street, "hook, hook," which meant the police were coming. The term "hook" came from the idea of someone calling the police, so that they knew the phone was off the hook. Another term that was commonly used for the police coming was "Five-O," which came from the television series Hawaii Five-O.

I knew I didn't have any drugs on me, so I didn't panic. Before I knew it, they had rushed into the store and snatched me out of there. I didn't find out until later when we went to court that the police had set up a surveillance team in an abandoned building in the middle of the block and had seen all of my transactions.

They practically drug me to my car and told me to open the trunk. I told them that I didn't have a key. I had it in top of my sock on the key ring. The police busted out my lock on the trunk, lifted up the spare tire, and took the bundles and my pistol. I was searched, handcuffed and taken down to the First Precinct. After we arrived at the station one of the detectives on the drug squad searched me thoroughly and found the key to the trunk in my sock. He looked at me and said, "Oh, you're going to pay m----- f-----, after having us to go through the trouble of busting in the car."

The police officer's partner came back and he told him that I had hidden the key. His partner who stood about 6'4,' told me, "When I get your little a— in the back, I'm going to knock the s--- out of you." They fingerprinted me, handcuffed me back up and escorted me to the back. Before I knew what happened that big joker hit me right in the face. I went flying back across the room, I hit the wall and slid down. They picked me up off the floor, removed the handcuffs and took me to a cell. It was morning, I had to wait until the next day to be arraigned on the charges. My head was hurting so badly that I slept for almost 24 hours until the next morning when I went to court.

I was charged with delivery of heroin, carrying a concealed weapon in the use of a felony and violation of probation. It didn't take long for me to go through the judicial system. I went to court twice, once for the arraignment and then for my preliminary examination. After the exam I took a cop or a plea bargain as the legal system refers to it. It turned out pretty good.

I tried to have the carrying concealed weapons during the commission of a felony charge lessened to an attempt to carrying a concealed weapon, since the gun was technically in the car and I wasn't in the car when I was arrested. I also tried to have the delivery of heroin lessened to a possession charge, as I was allowed to do twice, previously. I wanted the charges lessened in order to be eligible for probation again. Judge Kerwin had other plans for me. He told my attorney that he was not playing. In 1978, when he said that if I came again, I would without a doubt go to the State Prison in Jackson.

The delivery of heroin charge remained on my record in the event that I was arrested again on the same charge, it would be increasingly difficult for me. The CCW during a felony charge remained as well. The plea bargain gave me a suspended sentence on the delivery charge, but I had to do the mandatory two years for the weapons charge. I told others that I had my attorney to drive a hard bargain. Although, in reality, it was once again God looking out for me. I could have served a much longer sentence.

That was one of the shortest dope selling runs in my life. I started selling in August. I was busted in September, sentenced and sent to Jackson Prison in October. When I went for sentencing, I made sure that I took money with me so that my jail account would begin correctly. I had previously done short stays in the county jail and in the Detroit House of Corrections. I knew that on draw day I would be able to place an order with the jail commissary. I had to have money. However, after sentencing, I was to first go to the Wayne County Jail overnight and from there to Jackson. I put all my money in with my property. As it turned out, I ended up staying in the county jail for two weeks without any money to draw on because instead of it being in a jail account, it was in my property and the social worker never came to fill out the paperwork to transfer it. When it was time to transfer to Jackson Prison, I vowed that I would never do my time without money in hand to negotiate with. While on the van to Jackson, I took a few hundred-dollar bills, rolled them up tight, placed them in a thin plastic bag and coated them with Vaseline. I placed that money inside of me. It stayed there until I was in my cell in prison quarantine. Once I arrived to Jackson Prison, I was taken to the Reception and Guidance Center (RGC) before being placed in quarantine. It was that first stop when I was given a prison identity. I was now known as inmate number **162974.** This is the number that would identify me throughout the penal system. If I was to ever return, I would always remain **162974.** The only difference was the system would put a letter, B, C, D, etc. The letter that would precede the number, indicated how many times a prisoner has returned to the penal system.

I remained in quarantine for 21 days before being placed in general population or transferred to other prisons in the system. All the prison movies in the world cannot adequately prepare the first timer for the reality that hits you upon walking in the quarantine cell block for the first time. It is like an asylum for the criminally insane. Guys are hollering at the top of their lungs to each other and trying to intimidate the new "fish," which is what they called a new inmate coming into the system. They were looking for any signs of weakness. Including the base floor, there are five tiers with cells lined from one end to the other on both sides. While the prisoners were hollering, I was looking all the way up to the top and then looking all the way down to the end thinking, "Is this what I am going to be in the whole time? D------. I'd better sho'nuff put on my game face and not let my guard down for a second."

I was ushered to the center of the base floor to eat. I was eating and trying to make some sense of this hellish madness that I was to call my home for the next two years. I heard a distinct voice through all of the noise. It was something that was uplifting and fortifying to any inmate. It was the sound of my name, "Ricardo Thomas," being hollered loud by one of my homey's . It was Michael "Fish" Williams from Highland Park. "Hey, Crow" he shouted down to the base floor, where another guy from the hood was sweeping with a broom, "Rick Thomas is over there."

One of the first things that a person does when they go to prison is to look up other people they were cool with on the streets who are serving time. Needless to say, I was mobbed up real tight. There were quite a few guys that I knew from Highland Park in Jackson at the time. There was Fish, Crow, The Sandman, Tub, Charles, Leon, Willie, T-Bone, Butch Red, Howard, Billy and others; that was security.

After talking with Crow for a while, I got settled in my cell. All of the cells in Jackson on the south side were the same. The cells consisted of a bunk, toilet and sink. The ones in general population had a small locker as well. I had Crow to exchange one of the $100 bills that I smuggled in with me for prison tokens. The rate of exchange was a $100 bill for a 120 prison tokens. I had him to buy me some weed. As a janitor, he had mobility to go all over the cellblock, which provided him the opportunity to be in the loop to do plenty of hustling and make money. Just because a criminal is locked up doesn't mean that he quits hustling. We just had to play by a stricter set of rules because the guards were constantly around.

When Crow got back with my weed, I was shocked. I gave him five tokens, each token was worth a dollar, and he brought me back three toothpick size joints. "What is this Crow?" He answered, "That's how weed is in the joint, you don't get as much as on the streets. You pay two dollars for a thin joint but you could get a discount if you spend more money." I made up my mind from that day forth that I would find a way to start selling weed while I was locked up.

I was assigned to 16 block, tier D cell 27. Because of my skills in carpentry, I was assigned to work in the maintenance department as a carpenter. I had what was considered one of the best jobs in the system and made $1.10 a day. You had to hustle to maintain a certain lifestyle or be supported by family and friends who would send you money orders on a regular basis, because the money earned would not afford you much of anything but a few packs of cigarettes and very basic neccessities. I took advantage of the time that I had by taking college courses that Jackson Community College offered.

I was fortunate. My family visited me on a regular basis, bought me clothes and sent money. There was still something inside of me that wouldn't let me leave that criminal lifestyle alone.

The crew that I was on did all of the carpentry work in the Trustee Division and Parole Camp as well as the outlining farms. I was able to move weed for people throughout the prison system because of my mobility. I eventually hired others on the plumbing and electrical crews as well to move product. All I had to do now was get some product of my own.

I got a visit from my two brothers, Morris Jr. and Tony. I was telling them that I needed to get me some weed because I could make plenty of money while I was locked up. Tony, who played the guitar very well, was playing with George Clinton and the Parliament-Funkadelics band. He said to me, "Well , man, I got an ounce out in the car, let me go and get it for you." He started to get up and go to the car. I had to grab him and sit him down. I explained that it didn't work like that. We all fell out laughing when I explained the searches that took place after our visits. I told him that it would take me a while to connect with the right people to move weight. Guys would get little bags, pills, or heroin in balloons on visits that they would swallow, but I wanted to deal in larger quantities and had to learn the right procedures.

Six months later, I was transferred to Camp Waterloo in Grass Lake, Michigan, because of prison overcrowding conditions in the penal system. They had mass mobilization where they were shipping us out by the bus loads. There were over 300 of us sleeping in bunk beds in the gym waiting to be assigned to various prison camps. Camp Waterloo was the hub of the camp system. Everyone that was sent to a camp had to come through Waterloo before being shipped out.

I was assigned to stay at Waterloo and to the carpentry crew of the maintenance department. We did the carpentry work at all of the camps in the area. Either I or someone on one of the other crew would be at any of the camps throughout the week. I was now able to implement my plan to make some money. I had marijuana smuggled in and had a distribution network that not only operated at Camp Waterloo, but throughout the entire camp system. My number one enforcer was "Ace" Stone, who worked on the electrical crew. He was from the North End area of Detroit. Ace was over six feet tall and solid. He had no qualms about enforcing, intimidating, or inflicting pain if necessary. He was doing a bit for armed robbery and had five years in at the time. He had been locked up in one of the old prisons in the system called Ionia. A newer facility would later replace it. This is where they sent younger inmates from 18 to 22 to start their time. Everybody called it the "Gladiator School" This is where reputations were made and hierarchy established for those that were not already connected to groups. I also had him in charge of "the store" and "two for one" operations. We would buy cartons of cigarettes, which cost us .50 cents a pack. We sold them for $1.00 a pack. We made a hundred percent profit. Inmates that didn't have money in between draw days would come to us to borrow money, which we loaned "two for one." They would borrow $1.00 and when draw day came, they would have to pay back $2.00. That was a one hundred percent interest or profit. We would have someone in the office to keep us informed on the inmates outdates and transfers, so that an inmate would not think he was slick and borrow money from us and then leave before we were able to collect.

With the tokens collected from marijuana sells and other operations we had going, we bought green money (regular currency) from other inmates who were able to get it inside after a visit. I spent a lot of my evening hours in the arts and craft room building jewelry boxes with secret compartments to send home to relatives. Unbeknownst to them, I hid money in some of the jewelry boxes to be retrieved upon my release. I also sold jewelry boxes to other inmates to give as presents to their family, women and friends. I made greeting cards as well that would give Hallmark a run for there money. I made them out of manila file folders and draw pictures on them of flowers or erotic poses . I would then take pen to paper and write poetry that would bring smiles or tears depending on the occasion. I still write love poems today. I always hustled and was gifted with an entrepreneurial spirit. I had a saying, "Me and money ain't fell out." I also would send money home and have money orders sent to my supplier. They would send me my shipments. I had hooked up with some other inmates that would smuggle my shipment in for a fee. This was a nice arrangement. I smoked weed daily and drunk alcohol on occasion while I was at Camp Waterloo. I still did not consider myself an addict, because I was no longer using heroin. This is the misconception that a lot of people have, that weed and alcohol are not drugs.

The two are substances that are mood and mind altering chemicals that may cause individuals to become dependent upon them. Not realizing that I was still caught up, I turned to an older prisoner, K.C., and I asked him, "How does a person that has been locked up for years without using heroin, go back home and end up using again? I don't understand it." He just looked at me and smiled. Then he said, "It's very, very easy. Some would use the same day they hit the streets. For others it may take a little longer, but they eventually start back." The sound of his words caused me to shutter, thinking that I, too, may go back to shooting heroin.

K.C. worked on a crew that went out every day to another prison that had two facilities in one location. There was Ypsilanti Maximum prison for the men and Huron Valley for Women. The crew did landscaping and trash pickups. The great thing about this job was they worked alongside women inmates who had a short time remaining; that were allowed to work on the outside grounds. When one of the crew got busted for having sex with a female prisoner, KC got me a job with the crew. We looked forward to going to work EVERY DAY. I eventually hooked up with Jackie, a booster, (a real good thief) who was doing time for larceny at the women's prison at Huron Valley. The women's prison gave me another outlet to sale marijuana and Jackie ran that part of the operation for me.

I was called for over the loudspeaker one morning and was informed that I had received a ticket, which is an infraction of prison rules or policy. Someone had snitched on me. The office had been informed that I was sending money out in the mail. They intercepted and opened my mail one night, it was from the outgoing mailbox and they found green money that I was sending to Detroit. I was informed that I would be on the next bus going up North and that I was being sent to Camp Sauble up in Freesoil, Michigan. I had a few days left before the bus would be leaving to head up north. I had Ace to settle accounts right on the spot for 75 cents on the dollar. Those that were not able to pay, I turned their accounts over to Ace as a bonus for his loyalty so that he would still have money coming in after I was gone. I started packing for the trip. I left an ounce of marijuana with Ace and took the rest with me. I had it in a couple of my jewelry boxes, inside my TV, and another inmate that was being shipped out to Camp Sauble with me, carry some on him.

Once I arrived at Camp Sauble, I began to get settled in. One of the inmates that I traveled with, the one that smuggled the marijuana for me, walked around to see how the place was laying. I found out that another Highland Parker, Gregory Dowdell, was doing his time there also. We knew each other from the streets, but we never hustled or hung together. He was the "Mayor" of Sauble. In other words, he ran things up there. We learned that it was their draw day and they hadn't had any product for the last month. It was totally dry. We immediately set up shop and started selling. I gave my homey, Dowdell, an ounce. I did this for two reasons. One, he was a Highland Parker and you always looked out for your homeboys. They were eventually the ones that would go down with you if you ever had a beef with anybody or some drama took place. Secondly, I gave him his respect as the Mayor of the Sauble. It showed the other inmates that he was connected and still remained the man. That evening, Dowdell and I went walking on the "back forty." The term "back forty," was used to describe the rear yard of a prison, where the inmates would walk, play cards, lift weights, play basketball, etc. I would occasionally chip golf balls or ran. I began to love running and could do it for at least an hour or more at a time. You get to be in good shape in jail.

Dowdell told me that he would never forget what I did for him that day. I told him to think nothing of it, we were who we were, "thoroughbreds," and we do what we are supposed to do. My "out date," as the system calls it the day an inmate is released from prison, was four months away. I chilled for the rest of my bit. My father and mother visited me while I was up north. We had property in a place called Idlewild, Michigan, which used to be the black Mecca for summer vacations before integration. We would spend time there in the summer and around deer hunting season every year. Blacks from all over the Midwest, Detroit, Chicago, Cleveland etc, would come and vacation there. Many owned houses and cabins in and around the area. So a couple of times that summer when they came to spend time there, they took the one-hour ride over to see me.

Chapter 15

FREE AT LAST? NOT!

I was discharged from prison in September of 1982. I thought I was indeed free at last now that I was discharged from prison. I had no idea that I would soon become a prisoner of my former lifestyle. My father, Bishop, came to take me home. He never turned his back on me. He wouldn't condone my lifestyle, but he never denied me as his son. They had moved off of Doris and now lived in a larger home on Tuxedo near Second, in Highland Park. There was a room waiting for me. However, the prodigal son was not coming home to stay, it was just a visit; I hadn't come to my senses yet.

A month after I got home, I was back to shooting heroin and even smoking cocaine. I started smoking cocaine, the very thing that I said I was stupid six years earlier when I was in Los Angeles. I thought about what K.C. had told me in prison. "It's easy to go back." The Bible says in Proverbs, Like a dog going back to his vomit, a fool goes back to his folly.

Jackie came home from Huron Valley a month after I got out. By Thanksgiving she was back to boosting, and I was driving her to the malls. I soon got spoiled and accustomed to this way of living. Over the next few years we did this in between her going back to jail for new cases. When Jackie was locked up, I would go back to con hustles, like the "Box Game." We would place a broken TV in a good box and sell it as if it were stolen merchandise. I would work the "Loading Dock" scam with K.C. who was out of prison now and some other guys that had it down to a fine art. We would approach a person in the appliance or furniture department of Sears or some other store, and ask them what they were interested in purchasing. We would wear a smock or work uniform with a clipboard. We would tell the "mark," which was the person being conned, that someone had put that same item in lay-a-way; however, they had never came to claim it. For a discount they could purchase the item. All they had to do was give a fraction of the money now, so the lay-a-way could be taken care of, and we would give them their merchandise in the back at the loading dock. Needless to say, when the person went to the loading dock, they would be waiting a while before they realized they had been conned.

One who knows the mastery of the con game knows that real con is not played, it is executed. It takes place in such a way the "mark" has no idea how it all came about or when. They realize, usually when their money, valuables, or possessions are gone or their feelings are in disarray, that they have been had, bamboozled, totally violated and hung out in the wind. A con man has the gift of gab, as we called it, with the ability to manipulate and influence people to do your will without them even realizing it. Timing and signals through words or gestures with your partners all come into play in being successful.

During this time, I met another young lady. We also stayed together and my daughter Dominique was born on September 11th, 1985. I had left my father's house again because of the lifestyle I chose to live.

By 1986, I had plenty of friends who were smoking cocaine who would come over when they copped. I figured I should take advantage of the situation and started dealing again. I was selling to friends at first to support my own using. While I was on my way to pick up a package, I ran into Dowdell. Dowdell was the homey that I had befriended when I was locked up at Camp Sauble, and he told me that he was handling a little weight. So I started copping from him. He told me that he hadn't forgotten how I had looked out for him while we were locked up together. His appreciation was shown by his generosity.

Dowdell would always encourage me to take heavier weight. He would tell me when I didn't have the money that I could get it on consignment because I was good for it. I was satisfied with just getting an eighth of a kilo every other day. There was a Lifer's Law on the books in the State of Michigan and they were using it. People that were busted with too much weight were getting life sentences without parole. Judge Kerwin had made the last delivery permanent on my record; and, I knew that I would be facing 20 years to life if I were busted with a substantial amount of weight. There were a couple of things that I knew. One, I could go to jail and two, I could make money while I was in jail. However, anybody that does time can tell you that a prison is "No place to be somebody". It doesn't matter how much money you make locked up, you would trade it in a minute just to have your freedom.

Dowdell stayed my main connection until he died four years later. I was still smoking at this time as well, and the more I had, the more I would party. This was the main reason that my operation didn't get any larger. Partying with the product was bad business.

The operation was headquartered at my brother, Tony's house. He was still living in the house on Doris that we had grew up in. Tony was down with me all the way. Even today, people will see me and ask me how is Tony. He has cleaned up his life somewhat and works for the city. I still pray that he eventually will work with me in the Kingdom of God like we worked together for the Evil One. Sometimes we would go on runs and people would see him with his guitar case and think nothing of it since he was a musician. What they didn't know was instead of a guitar there would be a weapon inside. We had a large

125

entourage of people that hung around. There were friends that saw an opportunity to make some money. If they hadn't fallen out with money, then I allowed them the opportunity to make some. Then there were some that were there only for the drug lifestyle, parties and excitement. I had another lady that I was going with that hung tight and was down with me at the time, "Cimp" we got together around 1986 or 87.

This period of selling drugs was a wild time in my life. Cocaine causes people to act in ways that weed and heroin doesn't. There is a lust spirit that attaches itself to cocaine and people are addicted to it as well. The spirit will have you doing shameful and degrading acts. Never say "never" when you're hooked on drugs. People will come around and be willing to do the most embarrassing acts to get cocaine. There were episodes during my sadistic behavior when I would have women bark like a dog or tell them to mimic a chicken. There were marathon sessions that lasted for days at a time, consisting of orgies and all sorts of debauchery. Humiliating moments when we would make a complete fool of ourselves and not even be aware of it or care. Our behavior was self-centered; we were trying to satisfy a craving that could never be satisfied. As dopefiends, addicted to cocaine, we all shared in this way of life.

Another reason why our business on Doris

blossomed so well was because we saw to it that the customers who were interested in getting their sexual fantasies met had a place to fulfill them. They would make their request known, and we would provide them with the appropriate partner or partners. Women hung around hoping that they would be chosen to fulfill someone's fantasy, because it meant that they would be smoking cocaine soon thereafter. Never mind the degrading acts that had to be carried out. Often the female customers wanted to be fulfilled sexually in various ways as well. We accommodated them also.

In the streets, I was known as "Montebelli." Some people never even knew my real name Ricardo. This name was a combination of the actor, Ricardo Montabalm who was smooth and debonair, and Machiavelli, the 15th century Italian member of the royal court of the Medici Family. Machiavelli was the writer of the book "The Prince" It was about the skullduggery and manipulation of those in government and control. As I mentioned earlier, this was a very sadistic period in my life. I was really dissatisfied with myself and didn't mind inflicting pain on, and toward, others. It was as if I had become someone else entirely. Someone I didn't know. It was this persona that I took on in order to live with myself for the horrific deeds that I was committing. I eventually had to be delivered and inner healed. I tell people now that there is nothing too hard for

God and nothing that can be or could have been involved in that is so bad that God will not forgive you.

I discovered the blackouts that alcoholics experienced were not just passing out drunk. They were actually periods of time in which I functioned under the influence, usually exhibiting bad actions, after which I had no memory of the terrible things I had done or said to people. It seemed as though I lost a few days. As a matter of fact, I remember seeing an old movie "The Lost Weekend" featuring Ray Malland. In the movie, he played an alcoholic that went through the same behavior on a weekend binge.

When I didn't go home, I would stay at all the motels that were located up and down Woodward Avenue. As a matter of fact, I had moved into a motel when we got the word that the house on Doris was going to be raided. We got it from two reliable sources, one a police officer that we knew and the other from God. Really, what happened was my mother came over to the house and told everybody in there to come out on the porch. She then told us "I don't know what all you are doing in that house but God told me to tell you that you better stop and get out because something is about to happen." I knew enough and had enough sense that when my mother who flowed in the gift of prophecy said "God Said" you better pay attention. I told everyone who wanted to go, that I would pay for their motel rooms. Some stayed behind and were busted in the house including my brother, Tony. I had to post bond for five people that next day.

Before the police came in, we had moved all of the stolen merchandise that we bought from customers out of the house. When the police came in, "Montebelli" was no where to be found.

Chapter 16

THE DOWNWARD SPIRAL

Around the mid 1980's, Bishop's health began to fail. He had a heart attack and minor strokes. After his last stroke, he was paralyzed on one side of his body and lost the ability to talk. I would sit on the side of his bed or in the room in a chair and pour my heart out to him. I wanted to reassure him that the many life lessons he taught me were not in vain.

Often parents with wayward children ask themselves the haunting question, "Where did I go wrong?" Or they condemn themselves with the thought and/or declaration that they were bad parents. Usually more often than not, parents have done all they know to do, even according to scripture; but the child is rebellious and/or disobedient. The path the child chooses, whether they live or die, is because it is their choice and theirs alone. Parents need to free themselves of the guilt they tend to carry. There will understandably be feelings of sorrow and disappointment. However, feelings of guilt and condemnation should not linger, this is not of God.

Bishop died November 30, 1989 and from that point, my life began a more intensive downward spiral. I didn't understand it then but reflecting back, I recognize what happened. Something inside of me died when he died. I wasn't able to grieve until three years later. It was as if a light had gone out. What I felt was the one person that I wanted to be proud of me, more than anyone else, would never see his dream manifest; his dream to see his son off drugs and serving the Lord with him in ministry.

I realized years later why. When I would talk to him on his bed of affliction, he would cry and smile at me and pat my hand. I realize that he saw and knew something that I didn't. He always said that God had shown and promised him that I would be in the ministry. That is why when I think of him, I think of father Abraham and the scripture:

Romans 4:20-21
20   He staggered not at the promise of God through unbelief; but was strong in faith, giving glory to God;
21   And being fully persuaded that, what he had promised, he was able also to perform. (KJV)

Bishop knew that God was able to perform what He had promised, even if he was not alive to see it. He had received a good report through his faith; it just was not time for the manifestation in my life.

With my father dead, I lived a life that was disgusting even to me. I heard people talk about the muck and the mire. I decided to look up the definition of "mire." It is an area of wet, bog, deep mud that causes one to be entangled, sink or stick. I was definitely in the muck and the mire, because I was in a deep stinking lifestyle. I was entangled, caught up, mixed up, messed up, stuck and sinking.

I set up shop in a four-family flat on North Street, located near Log Cabin. It was drama from day one. There was someone across the hall that was selling cocaine off and on in small quantities. There were words exchanged between the guy whose flat I was using and the brother of the guy across the hall. It was getting heated and started to escalate. I called a meeting with the guy in charge and we quickly came to terms. I knew that business in the streets was no different from business in the corporate world. If you deal with people that were not hot heads and they have a real sense of business, they can always be met when there is something beneficial for all parties involved.

"Cimp", eventually moved into the flat upstairs over the joint. This was convenient for business, social and personal activities. There was another group of dealers that had a problem with us being in the neighborhood. They had a joint on Log Cabin that we constantly had to be on the look out for.

One evening I was standing in the dining room in the joint on North. Sitting at the dining room table were two guys, Spade and Chico, a player that lived in Palmer Park. While we were talking, the rapid sounds of an AK-47 rung out. Bullets came pouring in through the front windows of the flat. It seemed as if the sound would never end. When the shooting stopped, I was under the table against a wall. Spade had jumped behind a couch on the other side of the room, and Rico was in the back bedroom. "Cimp" was upstairs in her flat on the floor. We all stayed motionless and quiet for a very long time. We all sensed and heard that someone was walking around listening for inside movement and would start another assault. Finally, "Cimp" thumped on the floor of her flat and asked if we were all right. Miraculously, no one was hit. When I looked at the dining room wall where I was standing, there were bullet holes in the shape of a head. It was God's protection once again that kept me alive. Bullets hit and penetrated the wall all around my head and not a one hit me.

In real life, guns and the damage caused by them are not as neat as they are portrayed on TV or the movies. They show people running behind doors or furniture for protection. Bullets can go through doors, walls and furniture. The bullets that were fired into the flat were found in the back bedroom; they had gone through several walls. A bullet can enter a person's body making a small hole, but the exit wound can leave half their head torn off or a gaping hole in their back. I was yet alive because of God's mercy.

Later, I was informed that a contract was out on me, and I was "persona non grata" ,a person not wanted in the neighborhood. As Kenny Rogers says, "a gambler knows when to hold them and when to fold them." It was time for me to fold. I didn't have the backup or the organization at that time to retaliate. You have to pick your battles.

I was alternating my residences at the time. Sometimes I would stay in the Brightmoor area of Detroit in a nice house on Trinity with my baby girl Dominique and her mother. Or I would stay in an apartment with "Cimp". I had begun to feel very shameful when I would get high at home on Trinity. I would come into the house and head straight to the bedroom to smoke my cocaine. Dominique, who was about five years old at the time, would ask me questions the way children do when their father comes home. I would listen for a moment and then tell her that I would be right back; I had to take care of my business. One particular day when I walked in the front door, she made a statement in the form of a question. She said "Daddy, I know you have to go take care of your business and then you will come and talk to me, right?" When I went into the bedroom to get high, I cried all while I smoked my cocaine. My baby daughter, knew that there was something in my life that always came before her.

Luke 15:14-16

14   After he had spent everything, there was a severe famine in that whole country, and he began to be in need.

15   So he went and hired himself out to a citizen of that country, who sent him to his fields to feed pigs.

16   He longed to fill his stomach with the pods that the pigs were eating, but no one gave him anything. (NIV)

"Cimp" and I had stayed in various apartments all over the west side of Detroit, but the last place was the pits. We were staying in an apartment building at 60 Highland, in Highland Park, which was drug-infested. I wasn't selling dope, I was only using. We slept on a mattress on the floor that we took and drug down the alley in the winter snow. We shared the apartment with another family, the "Roaches." In two years, I had gone from selling ounces of cocaine, drinking Hennessey all day and smoking on the biggest cocaine pipe made at the time, to living in a roach and drug infested apartment building. I was drinking half-pints of Nikolai Vodka or Wild Irish Rose wine and smoking kibbles and bits which we called small pieces of cocaine.

Just like the prodigal son who came to his senses and went back home, during the summer of 1991, I was sick and tired of being sick and tired. I finally realized that I needed help in a bad way. I began to hear over and over in my mind the voice of my father and mother, "You're living beneath your God-given privileges." I knew I needed help, but I was not able to stop using the drugs on my own. I had tried on numerous occasions. I was yet addicted to cigarettes, crack cocaine and alcohol. I had quit using heroin in 1987.   I would go by my mother's house to visit, usually when I needed some money. While I was visiting, when she was not on the first floor with me, I would go into her kitchen and steal food. I would be too ashamed to let her know that I was hungry. I didn't want her to know that I wasted my money on drugs before I would buy food. Ma Dear would say to me often that my butt would have to be dragging the ground before I gave up my lifestyle of selling and using. I would get so angry with her when she would say that. I accused her of burning bread on me, which meant to place a curse on someone. However, she was telling the truth; I would have to hit rock bottom before I would become willing to look up for help.

I had a camera that I was taking to the pawnshop. I was at the bus stop on Woodward and Glendale when a friend of mine, that I used to get high with, walked up. It was Dana Kennedy and his fiancée Pamela. We were all getting on the same bus. He began to witness to me, telling me that he was clean and sober. He was attending Narcotics Anonymous meetings. He told me what was most important to him was the fact that he was now a Christian, in the church and actually born again. I was amazed. He was also attending service with After Christ, a ministry held in a church where meetings were based on a 12-Step Program, much like Alcoholics for Christ. It was strictly God and Christ centered. Dana said that Robert (Rubby Tub) Payne was also a Christian now. I listened, but in the back of my mind I was thinking about the pawnshop and the money I was going to get for the camera, so that I could get high.

As it turned out, the pawnshop closed at 12:00 p.m. on Thursdays and I had forgotten. I had to catch the bus all the way home from downtown. I knew I wouldn't get the money the camera was worth from the dope man that I could have gotten at the pawnshop. The bus trip gave me time to think about what Dana said about being a Christian. The seed of God's word that had been planted inside of me during childhood was being watered.

Chapter 17

PART II

Redemption, Reconciliation & Restoration

Colossians 1:19-22
19   For God was pleased to have all his fullness dwell in him,
20   and through him to reconcile to himself all things, whether things on earth or things in heaven, by making peace through his blood, shed on the cross.
21   Once you were alienated from God and were enemies in your minds because of your evil behavior.
22   But now he has reconciled you by Christ's physical body through death to present you holy in his sight, without blemish and free from accusation (NIV)

God in His infinite wisdom knew that humanity would be in a sinful state and separated from Him. He therefore made a provision for all of us to be reconciled back to Him through Jesus Christ, His Son. It is because of the definitive work on the cross at Calvary; the death, burial and resurrection of Christ, which is the gospel according to scripture that we are able to receive salvation and be redeemed. God is longsuffering toward us and His desire is that none of us should perish but live life eternal with Him.

John 3:15-16

15   That whosoever believeth in him should not perish, but have eternal life.

16   For God so loved the world, that he gave his only begotten Son, that whosoever believeth in him should not perish, but have everlasting life.(KJV)

The second part of this book depicts the love of God as strong and powerful. He extends his grace and mercy upon anyone that repents, asks for forgiveness, and accepts Jesus Christ. God can redeem, reconcile and restore the life of anyone. Don't think that your life has been so sin ridden that God doesn't love you. He did it for my life because He is faithful. The faithfulness of God is such that when you are at your lowest, when you are at your weakest point in life, God's grace can come in and make you strong and enable you to come out of any addictive lifestyle or negative behavior.

Chapter 18

LOOKING FOR RELIEF

I went to the City of Detroit's Health Department, Herman Kiefer Hospital to sign up to enter a treatment center in August of 1991. I was 39 years old and had been getting high since I was 14 years of age. I chose the treatment center as opposed to an outpatient facility, because I knew that in an outpatient program, where I would be out in the streets everyday I would get high. I was not strong enough for an outpatient program.

I reported to the Elmhurst Home in three days, they had a bed available for me. It was located on the corner of Elmhurst and Linwood. Ironically, it was right in an area that I used to get plenty high. It was also around the corner from my ex-girlfriend Jackie, the booster.

I knew of people that were delivered from drugs. They went for prayer and asked God for deliverance and they were delivered from drugs immediately. However, they had the faith to believe that it could be done. I, on the other hand, did not possess this type of faith. I just knew I needed help. My relationship with God was such that I wasn't thinking of God delivering me. Nevertheless, at times I would lie down at night and ask God to take the desire away from me because I was so tired of the way I was living my life.

I decided not to tell my lady who I was staying with at the time that I was going into a treatment center. The day that I was assigned to go into treatment, I waited until she went to work and I left. I loaded up the television and VCR in the car and went to the pawnshop. I was going to have one more for the road before I went into the treatment center. Remember, during this time I only had a desire to change; I hadn't changed yet. I was still a self-centered, crack addict that would justify anything for the cause of satisfying my bottomless cravings for drugs. I wasn't concerned at the time about how she would feel when she came home and didn't have a television. People that say, "I'd never do that," haven't used drugs long enough. I was in a state of moral and spiritual bankruptcy.

After getting the money I hurried to my brother, Tony's house to get high. I ended up walking my high, drunk, self into Elmhurst Home on August 14, 1991. When I walked in the door, one of the people that greeted me was Marshall, who had grown up in Highland Park, as well. He had lived a notorious life and was someone that people should have written off as not amounting to anything but a gangster. Marshall was an employee at Elmhurst, studying to be a substance abuse counselor, and most important had accepted salvation, and was attending church. Dana was the first person that I had been in the streets with and I saw a change. Now here was Marshall. I really was beginning to believe more and more that there was hope for me.

Once I was in the treatment center, it took about a week to adjust to not getting high every day. The fog was starting to lift from my mind, and I allowed myself to listen to the messages that were given. The messages were taken from the 12-Steps of N.A. (Narcotics Anonymous). The N.A. program was based on spiritual principles. I had come to the realization that what they were advocating here in this 12-Step Program is nothing different from what I had been hearing my entire young life in the church; scripture and biblical principles. I eventually studied and began following the Alcoholics for Christ literature, because they strictly used biblical scripture to support each step, rather than a generic "god of your choice or any higher power."

During that first week and a half in Elmhurst, a dreaded fear seemed to overwhelm me. I didn't share it with anyone but before I went into Elmhurst Home, I had to have a complete physical done by the City of Detroit Department of Health. The physical included a complete blood work and this was the first time that I was tested for HIV. I was given a number to call the Department of Health in 10 days and the nurse would tell me if my testing was negative or positive. It was during those 10 days that I constantly reflected on my lifestyle and the, too numerous to count, sex partners that I had personally and also shared with others. At the time, I was caught up in a sexual addiction as well a drug addiction. I wasn't concerned with where a woman had been, as long as she was fulfilling my lustful desires and my pornographic fantasies were being met.

When I made the call to the Department of Health, I was nervous. I was cursing myself for being so reckless and cavalier with my life, having unprotected sex. I knew I couldn't blame it on anyone but myself if I was infected with the HIV virus. If I had to name partners, I knew that I couldn't remember them all or where to locate many of them. I was a wreck.

"NEGATIVE." When I heard those words spoken over the phone by the nurse, it was as if someone had given me a pardon from a guilty verdict and facing a death sentence. I did thank God. However, it wasn't until I accepted Jesus Christ as my Lord and Savior that I really understood that it was God that protected me all along. There were many of my associates, within the next ten years that were going to die from AIDS. I would sit and visit with them in their hospital rooms, seeing the disintegration of their bodies. In between the laughter, tears and prayers I would remember so often thinking

"This very well could have been me". There were many people that I had shared needles with before the HIV pandemic in the 80's. After that I refused to share needles. I would use my own set of works (needles and syringe) to get high with, but I still engaged in unprotected sex.

The Elmhurst Home, like other rehabilitation facilities, tell the participants in treatment that only two out of ten will make it. This statement is frightening, yet it is based on actual statistics. As a result, I began to experience a variety of mixed feelings. Some people think, "What's the use in being here, I really don't have a chance." Others make affirming statements as, "Well, I bet I will be one of the two." I can attest that if an individual has a true personal relationship with Christ they have hope to believe they can do all things, including staying clean from alcohol and drugs.

While I was in treatment, I met many who had been in treatment at least five times. I wondered if this would be the pattern for me as well. I had been in at least ten methadone clinics all over the city, through both private and the Department of Health. This is why I insisted on in-patient. In-patient treatment helped me to reach a point where I was able to have a clear head and heart to rededicate my life to Christ and truly accept Him as my Higher Power.

Romans 13:1
Let every soul be subject unto the higher powers.
For there is no power but of God: the powers that
be are ordained of God. (KJV)

Chapter 19

GOD CALLS US AND DRAWS US

Jeremiah 31:33
The LORD appeared to us in the past, saying: "I have loved you with an everlasting love; I have drawn you with loving-kindness. (NIV)

When we are not aware of it, God is drawing us to Him. I went into the treatment center with one agenda, which was to be admitted for 30 days, get clean, come out and return to my glory filled days of selling dope. This time, I would stack up my money and have something to show for it. My agenda was to quit using, not quit selling.

God had a different plan in mind. Oftentimes, we have a specific agenda or plan and God comes along and interrupts, upsets, or turns our entire plan around. God will use situations and circumstances to get our attention, which is exactly what happened to me when I went into the treatment center. I was minding my own business, without a thought of being reconciled with God. This is the way that God does things. When it comes to saving the lives of those that are lost, God will snatch them out prior to destruction. He loves us so much that he sent Christ so that we would not be condemned and perish, but have eternal life.

I thought that I had to "get right" first, before I came back to God. I knew that I was not in shape to be a Christian. I didn't feel that I was able to live that type of lifestyle. I didn't realize that all I had to do was accept Christ as my Lord and Savior and God would clean me up; and, the Holy Spirit would help me to live a Godly life.

The Apostle Paul also had his own agenda. He was doing in his life what he always did. While he was known as Saul of Tarsus, riding on the road to Damascus to arrest and kill Christians, the plan was changed. On the road, he was knocked off his horse and he received a revelation of who God really is. It was after God's intervention that he was able to understand what his true purpose in life was.

There is another example that comes to mind. When Jesus was walking along the seashore he saw Peter and his brother, Andrew. They, too, were going about their everyday routine of fishing and casting nets. Jesus spoke to them and told them, "Follow me, and I will make you fishers of men." These were men that received revelation quickly. In Matthew 4:20 and in Mark 1:18 it reads that "straightway (immediately) they stopped what they were doing and followed Him." It took a while for me to develop the same faith and trust that Peter and Andrew had according to the book of Mark, Chapter I.

Mark 1:16-20.
16 As Jesus walked beside the Sea of Galilee, he saw Simon and his brother Andrew casting a net into the lake, for they were fishermen.
17 "Come, follow me," Jesus said, "and I will make you fishers of men."
18 At once they left their nets and followed him.
19 When he had gone a little farther, he saw James son of Zebedee and his brother John in a boat, preparing their nets.
20 Without delay he called them, and they left their father Zebedee in the boat with the hired men and followed him. (NIV)

I've heard people quote Mao Tse-Tung saying that "Religion is the opiate of the masses," or paraphrased as it is only for the poor and disenfranchised; those who have no hope or substantial means of support." However, in examining some of the men that Jesus called into the ministry as disciples, we see that they were men of substance and wealth. When Jesus called James and John, they were also in a ship mending their nets (Mark 1:19-20). They were part owners in a business with their father, and they also had employees. The Bible says they left their father, Zebedee, in the ship with the hired servants and followed Jesus.

Elisha was also a man of substance and wealth; he chose to follow the man of God, Elijah.

I Kings 19:19-21
So Elijah went from there and found Elisha son of Shaphat.He was plowing with twelve yoke   of oxen,

and he himself was driving the twelfth pair. Elijah went up to him and threw his cloak around him.

20   Elisha then left his oxen and ran after Elijah. "Let me kiss my father and mother good-by," he said, "and then I will come with you." "Go back," Elijah replied. "What have I done to you?"

21   So Elisha left him and went back. He took his yoke of oxen and slaughtered them. He burned the plowing equipment to cook the meat and gave it to the people, and they ate. Then he set out to follow Elijah and became his attendant. (NIV)

This scripture teaches that a relationship with God and living a life patterned after Jesus Christ is not just for the poor but for people of substance and money as well.

After getting into Elmhurst treatment center and hearing the messages, I realized I was going to stay longer than 30 days. I ended up being a resident there for 90 days. I attended classes daily, which were mandatory. I learned that true recovery is not to stop using drugs, but to change my attitude and behavior. Which is really what repenting is, a change of mind, from doing what was wrong to start doing what is right. The Bible instructs us to do just this in Ephesians.

Ephesians 4:22-28
22   You were taught, with regard to your former way of life, to put off your old self, which is being corrupted by its deceitful desires;
23   to be made new in the attitude of your minds;
24   and to put on the new self, created to be like God in true righteousness and holiness.

25 Therefore each of you must put off falsehood and speak truthfully to his neighbor, for we are all members of one body.
26 "In your anger do not sin": Do not let the sun go down while you are still angry,
27 and do not give the devil a foothold.
28 He who has been stealing must steal no longer, but must work, doing something useful with his own hands, that he may have something to share with those in need. (NIV)

I was beginning to feel God's love for me while in treatment. I began to reflect on the numerous times that I could have been murdered, dead or incarcerated for life. I received revelation that it was the grace and mercy of God that was extended to me. His mercy, in that He withheld the punishment that I so rightly deserved. His grace, in that He gave me the chance to live and be reconciled unto him.

Chapter 20

COMING TO MY SENSES

Luke 15:17-20
17   "When he came to his senses, he said, 'How many of my father's hired men have food to spare, and here I am starving to death!
18   I will set out and go back to my father and say to him: Father, I have sinned against heaven and against you.
19   I am no longer worthy to be called your son; make me like one of your hired men.'
20   So he got up and went to his father. "But while he was still a long way off, his father saw him and was filled with compassion for him; he ran to his son, threw his arms around him and kissed him. (NIV)

I finally began coming to my senses as the Prodigal Son did. After living for over 25 years high, addicted and depraved, I was beginning to realize that there was a better life. My heavenly Father, as well as my natural family, had many blessings in store for me; so much love to offer, and, yet I was denying myself the privilege of sharing in that love and comfort.

Many gain knowledge and some learn the principles; however, some lack the wisdom to act

151

accordingly. After coming to my senses, I had to make a decision and act. After coming to his senses, the Prodigal Son rose up and set out for his father's house. I did the same. I called my mother, who was pastoring the church after Bishop died. I told her that I would like to begin going to church on Sundays. I, too, as the Prodigal Son was afar, but began my journey in returning home. I wanted to come back home and express that, "I have been wrong, please forgive me." The following Sunday, she was there to pick me up for Service. After that first Sunday my mother, my brother-in-law, Dr. Robyn Haithcock, or Deacon Fred Westbrook Jr., would come and pick me up on Sunday mornings to attend church. Fred Westbrook Jr. had been delivered immediately from his addiction through prayer. He is now an Ordained Elder at Faith Tabernacle Church and oversees the Men's Ministry.

I was finally on my journey to my Father's House. When I was being released from treatment, I asked my brother, Mo, if I could live with him for a couple of months, until I got on my feet. His immediate response was "yes." Mo was not like the older brother in the Biblical story of the Prodigal Son. That older brother was angry that his brother was coming home to take his rightful place, and angry with their father who took great joy in his lost son coming home. Mo took me in, and the couple of months ultimately ended up being a couple of years. He stuck by me and supported me when I was going through that very difficult first year. I will always love my family.

Chapter 21

NOW WHAT?

For some, there is a season after answering God's call and accepting Christ as their Savior, that they ask the question "Now what?" Newly saved Christians often ask themselves, "Okay, now I'm saved, I'm in the church, now what?" They're accustomed to living a certain lifestyle that is ungodly; they were caught up in sin and suddenly they're instructed to give up cigarettes, sleeping around and much more. They find themselves saying and wondering, now what? Where do I go from here? I'm not smoking, now what? Now what am I supposed to do? I recall going through this ordeal when I recommitted my life to God. After services were over, I would question myself: "Now, what? I'm back in the church, Lord." At one point, I was singing in the choir but after church, after those few hours were over, my question again was, "Now what?" I had to go back out and face the world and there was emptiness inside. I was glad God was in my life, but I felt something was missing. I felt a void.

I would sit in the church after service and cry sometimes, because I didn't have anything to do and I felt as if I had nowhere to go. I couldn't go back to my old friends; they were all still getting high, doing the things that I was trying to get away from. I wasn't strong enough to visit my brother, Tony who eventually quit smoking cocaine. I still would love to see him active in serving the Lord. Some of our old friends would probably be there and I was afraid that if they invited me to hit the pipe or have a drink, I would probably give in. I had enough sense not to tempt myself because I knew that was a form of lust and I couldn't afford exposure to temptation. I did not want to satisfy my flesh and sin, so I avoided going in that direction. Again, I was asking, "now what?"

There were about seven or eight other guys from the treatment center that started going to church with me. Some became members. I was struggling during this period. We would all be together and I would ask, "Say, are you guys making it alright?" I can still hear the answers. "Yeah, I'm straight. Aw man, I ain't never going back, I'm through using for life." Here I was thinking that something was wrong with me. I didn't realize they were lying; we all were having some type of temptations, and giving in to them. As my father used to say, "It'll all come out in the wash, and what does not come out in the wash will come out in the rinse." I avoided them and dealt with the temptation for as long as I could. It wasn't long before I was sneaking around getting high, trying to keep it on the down low.

When someone is not rooted in the Word of God, it is easy to fall back into what's familiar and begin to associate with people from the past. In the first year, I relapsed. I tried to stay straight but I didn't know enough of the Word of God to remain delivered. I was struggling, as the Apostle Paul explains in the book of Romans, Chapter 7. I was saved and delivered, yet unspiritual. I was carnal-minded and found myself a slave to sin. The thing that I wanted to do, stay clean, sober and serve God, I was not doing. The things that I didn't want to do, I found myself doing again. I realized sin still had a grip on me although I was back in the church.

I'll never forget October 1992, during my first year in the church, I was sneaking out to cop and a guy I knew saw me and asked, "What are you doing here, Rick? You don't belong here." Getting flat out busted, I immediately went into my old behavior, I lied. "Oh, I'm just copping for this woman I have around the corner." He knew that I wasn't supposed to be there because I was professing to be a born again Christian. His words pierced right to the very core of my heart and spirit. I felt like Peter, my actions were denying Christ.

Yet the wretched man that I was, I cried out, "who will rescue me from this misery?" Jesus Christ, that's who!

Mo, whom I was living with wasn't naïve. He knew I was getting back into things I had no business doing. He didn't condone it, he continued to encourage me. He would encourage me by saying that I had to get it together, and that I could keep it together.

God answered one of my prayers. My sister, Lisa, and her new husband, Robyn Haithcock, began to invite me to dinner with them. I would go out and eat with them and it felt so good to belong with someone, to be able to socialize; to be a part. As a result, I am now able to recognize this is important for new saints in the body, they need fellowship; whether they come from an addicted background or not. They need to feel love, the sense of belonging, and being able to fellowship. If that need is not fulfilled, they will isolate themselves or go back to associating with old friends and familiar territory. Without realizing it, they will run the risk of falling back into their old lifestyles.

When I shared with Deacon Fred Westbrook, Jr. that I was struggling, he told me, "The Word will keep you delivered," I began to read more of the Word.

Matt 12:43-45
43   "When an evil spirit comes out of a man, it goes through arid places seeking rest and does not find it.
44   Then it says, 'I will return to the house I left.' When it arrives, it finds the house unoccupied, swept clean and put in order.

Then it goes and takes with it seven other spirits more wicked than itself, and they go in and live there. And the final condition of that man is worse than the first. That is how it will be with this wicked generation." (NIV)

That's how many Christians are. We've been cleaned up, swept, purged, delivered and set free from the things that had us bound. When the enemy comes back and finds the house not filled, that's when temptation is thrown our way. Temptation is stronger than what we're accustomed to resisting. This is why it is very important for all Christians to become saturated with the Word of God. One must be willing to put off old sinful ways and come into the Body of Christ, where we put on a new way of living. We must be saturated with the Word of God. We need to fill those voids with the Word of God, the things of God, the attributes of God, and the fruit of the Spirit, so that we're not easily prone to backslide and go to our old familiar ways, when faced with troubling situations and circumstances.

As a result of this experience, I developed and implemented a "New Membership" Class to teach Basic Bible Doctrine. The church also offers men and women discipleship classes, which are designed to help new Christians, become rooted and grounded in the Word of God and spiritually mature.

Chapter 22

REDEMPTION

Ps 107:1-2
1 O give thanks unto the LORD, for he is good: for his mercy endureth for ever.
2 Let the redeemed of the LORD say so, whom he hath redeemed from the hand of the enemy; (KJV)

I realize that God kept me alive through all of my sinful ways to allow me the opportunity to recommit my life to Him. He loved me so much that while I was still living contrary to His word, he already sent Christ to reconcile me back unto Him. Christ died that I might be redeemed.

Romans 5:8
8 But God commendeth his love toward us, in that, while we were yet sinners, Christ died for us. (KJV)

Being redeemed is like purchasing a valued item from a pawnshop. The item is sitting there, not being used. Yet it has value, worth and purpose. Any item without value and worth can't be pawned. Our lives have value, worth and purpose. Yet living a sinful life is as if the evil one is holding us in pawn. He wants to kill, steal and destroy us. He will trick us by fooling us into thinking we have no value or worth; that we have been so terrible that

God couldn't possibly love or want us. God's desire is that none of us perish but have everlasting life. God redeemed me. It was as if He came in with the pawn ticket and said, "I want Ricardo Thomas, I want to redeem him." The price for the life of Ricardo and all sinners that believe has been paid by Jesus Christ when he died on the cross. Christ died on the cross and shed his blood, that was the price for my redemption. The bill was stamped "PAID IN FULL." He retrieved me, and redeemed me, so that I could fulfill the purpose ordained for my life; using my talents and gifts to the honor and glory of God. I was a salesperson and businessman but instead of selling drugs and living sinful, I may live as an example and tell other people the benefits of God. God showed me that not only did I have the talent and gift to build and remodel houses, but I could be used by Him to help build other's lives.

I also discovered that I was not alone. There are many people who are "ex's" -- ex-drunkard, ex-dope fiend, ex-abuser, ex-something. You fill in the blanks. Every one has been saved from something. Some people have had to be saved from themselves. They were their own worse enemy.

> 1 Corinthians 6:9-11
> 9 Do you not know that the wicked will not inherit the kingdom of God? Do not be deceived: Neither the sexually immoral nor idolaters nor adulterers nor male prostitutes nor homosexual

offenders

10 nor thieves nor the greedy nor drunkards nor slanderers nor swindlers will inherit the kingdom of God.
11 And that is what some of you were. But you were washed, you were sanctified, you were justified in the name of the Lord Jesus Christ and by the Spirit of our God. (NIV)

I realize that when a person is in bondage he or she is not being used the way God desires for them to be used. In most cases, they're not being used at all. If they are being used, they're being misused or they're being abused.

The joy of coming from a self-centered life of an addict, user, and manipulator to a life that is God-centered is an unspeakable joy. I get full and shed tears of joy and happiness when I think that my life was spared for such a time as this. Christ paid the price and He paid it in full. Isaiah 53:5 says, "He was wounded for our transgressions, He was bruised for our iniquities and the chastisement of our peace was upon Him; and by His stripes we are healed." Because of Calvary, I was set free from the slavery of addiction.

I was grateful to be in the Body of Christ, back in the church that I had grown up in and ran away from. I came back relieved just to be in the door. I had no intentions or desire of working in the ministry. I was satisfied just being back in my Father's House. I use every opportunity that I

161

can to tell others about the redemptive power of God through Jesus Christ. Let the redeemed of the Lord say so. **I SAY SO !!!!!.**

When some one does something nice to us or for us, we have no problem with saying thank you. We will even tell others about the act of kindness that was bestowed on us. In that same mode of thinking, when we look back over our lives and as the song writer says, and we think things over, we can truly say that we've been blessed and we do indeed have a testimony. Without hesitation, we need to let the world know that Christ died for our sins, that we have been redeemed, we are forgiven and they have the same opportunity as well.

Chapter 23

FORGIVENESS

It is such a joy to realize that my past sins are forgiven, to understand God had blotted out my transgressions. I had to learn to forgive myself also, the way that God had forgiven me. It was not always easy to do. I would look back over my life and see the pain, hurt and heartache that I had caused people, and I was truly ashamed of my actions. God has forgiven me for those things that I thought were unforgivable. Things that people don't forgive each other for or are not in position to forgive you for because they are not around or no longer living. There are some things that will probably go to the grave with me. Only God and I know and some other people and they aren't telling. I had to go to others and ask their forgiveness for my actions. Some forgave me unconditionally. Others said they had to think about it. I was comforted in knowing that I did as the Bible instructed, to go to someone if you know or think that they hold something against you.

I went and asked for forgiveness as well from my children's mothers. I had been through and caused a lot of "the baby's mama" drama. I can honestly say that the three mothers of my five children did an excellent job of raising the children in my absence and sporadic attendance and involvement in our children's earlier years. When we speak the truth that a child never forgets, it encompasses both the positive as well as the negative. In viewing the negative aspects of it, a child can carry the emotional scars and painful memories of bad relationships or parental abandonment for life. Children never forget that Daddy wasn't always or never there. The effect can be physically, emotionally and spiritually damaging. Some children live in single parent homes. Yet some live in homes where both parents may be there physically but are never there to support, encourage or teach the children. As a result they too have scars, wounds and emotional damage.

Many people do not attend church or have a relationship with God because their parents did not have a relationship with God. It is very important that children have their parents take them to church and not send them to church. Proverbs 22:6 tells us to "train up a child in the way that he should go, and when he is old he will not depart from it."

A child remembers broken promises, whether made with good intentions or not. All they remember is that the promise was never fulfilled. For example, the bike or toy never received but promised, the trip to the movies or the ball game never attended. Perhaps, it was the walks never taken or the conversations that were always postponed for

164

one reason or another. There was the unspoken message that was given to my children that something or someone else was always more important than them. Maybe it was a missed birthday, holiday, recital, plays, school activities, church function or being together one on one; just you and me, activities were never attended for one reason or another.

I asked my children to forgive me. These were some very emotional, gut wrenching experiences for me. To say I was sorry for not being there or being the father that I was supposed to be. I told them that I could not correct the past, but I would be the father that I was meant to be from that day forward. The boys said "ok." Yet, I could sense the doubt and/or the attitude that I'll wait and see if he is lying or telling the truth. Tamara (Micki) is my oldest child, she was 16 years of age at the time and she wrote me a letter that I still have to this day, which reads:

> "Dear Dad,
> Dad, I'm just glad that you are finally seeking treatment. I pray to God it lasts. You don't have to feel ashamed anymore. What makes me ashamed is if you keep doing the same thing you used to do, but if I see you trying to do better, just to try I won't be ashamed. I understand that things happen and that there is a reason   for everything. I forgive you and I pray that you keep God first in everything you do.   R.M.A.
>
>   Tamara
>   BKA
>   Micki "

I thank God for the opportunity to be a part of my children's lives now. God has healed deep hurts and emotional scars in all of us. He has restored the relationships and is continuing to bond us closer.

Tamara has graduated from college with her Masters Degree, is a teacher and has been married to Courtney Lots. They have two beautiful children; a daughter, Kourtney and son, Ky-Lee. Two of my sons, Morris and Steven, have graduated from college and have completed grad school; Steven with a Masters in Chemical Engineering and Morris with a Ph.d. in Higher Education. Morris is now an author himself with a book titled "Focus" the missing factor to accomplishing goals. V. Ricardo Jr. is an ordained Evangelist , Praise and Worship Leader, songwriter and has served as the Minister of Music at Faith Tabernacle for many years before relocating to Chicago. Dominique, my youngest daughter, has graduated from Boston College. She even came and lived with Cynthia and I during some of her high school years. It was a joy for us to be able to shuttle her to school up in Bloomfield Hills every morning.

I not only had to ask others for forgiveness, I had to grant forgiveness to some as well. I understood that the same way that God had shown me his mercy, became necessary for me to show others. When He forgave me, it released me from the weighted feelings of guilt and shame that I had carried inside of me for many years. Being set free from those weights has enabled me to share my story with others as well. On occasion, I run into old friends and acquaintances and tell them of God's forgiveness. Some have given their lives to Christ and received salvation, some have gotten teary eyed and openly cried, while others tell me they are coming to church. I inform them that it is not about what church they attend or join, it is about having a relationship with Jesus Christ.

Chapter 24

RESTORATION

Once I came back to church in 1991 and struggled that year, I recommitted my life back to God in 1992. I was received at home with plenty of love. Although, my natural family was glad that I came home and back to the Lord, there were some people in the church that were like the Prodigal Son's older brother. Today, we call those types of people "Player Haters."

> Luke 15:25-30
> 25 "Meanwhile, the older son was in the field. When he came near the house, he heard music and dancing.
> 26 So he called one of the servants and asked him what was going on.
> 27 'Your brother has come,' he replied, 'and your father has killed the fattened calf because he has him back safe and sound.'
> 28 "The older brother became angry and refused to go in. So his father went out and pleaded with him.
> 29 But he answered his father, 'Look! All these years I've been slaving for you and never disobeyed your orders. Yet you never gave me even a young goat so I could celebrate with my friends.
> 30 But when this son of yours who has squandered your property with prostitutes comes home, you kill the fattened calf for him!' (NIV)

What if the father had not been home when the son returned? What if the brother that stayed behind was the one to greet him? What if it was that brother that had unforgiveness in his heart or some other servant that didn't like him that met him?. Having to deal with people that think like the older brother, will keep you and others outside the house and in the yard.

Satan's master plan is to destroy the kingdom of God by destroying the lives of those that are ordained to possess the kingdom. Satan loves for all of the prodigal sons and daughters to stay bound and caught up, and not return to their Father's house. If you do return, the evil one has people he uses to try to get you to leave the Father's House. Remember, it is your birthright, don't give it up.

There were brothers and sisters in the Body of Christ that were not happy at all that I had returned to my family. Everybody is not always glad that you are restored to your relationship with God. I remember people looking at me as if to say, "What are you doing here?" As if I wasn't worthy to be restored to a relationship with Christ because of my past and the way I had been living. I believe they actually felt as if I was beneath salvation or restoration. Oftentimes, when people accept Jesus Christ as their Lord and Savior, there are people in the Body of Christ that will look down on them with haughty eyes or turn their noses up as if they're less than. There is a perverse spirit of self righteousness, arrogance and entitlement that stinks in the nostrils of God in those type of people. They fail to realize that the Bible tells us that we are all sinners.

If it weren't for the grace of God and the fact that Christ died on the cross, none of us would be redeemed. He redeemed all of us. It's not that some are more worthy than others. The Bible tells us that we _all_ have sinned and come short of the glory of God. This is something that should be addressed in the Body of Christ because people have a tendency to think that they're better than others. This reminds me of the older brother in the Prodigal Son in the Bible. I imagine he was so angry that he began to tell people, "You know, I have been here all the time." That's often the way some people in the church feel. They feel that since they haven't "backslid," were raised in the church or perhaps because they stayed in the church with their hidden sins, or those that have not sinned since they were saved, they are superior. These Christians tend to get angry and/or frustrated. They tell God, "I've been here all the time, why are you restoring them?" God will speak to their spirit if they will listen. He says, "Hey, everything I have is yours, you had it all the time and this is the beauty of it all. Since you've been here all the time, everything that I have, you've been able to partake of and benefit from it, where the sinner has not."

When the sinner comes back, God wants to let them know that they're able to partake of the blessings as well and sit at the banquet table. The player haters in the church feel that the backslider or sinners shouldn't be allowed restoration. Once we come to know how God works, He often uses the most unlikely people to carry out his plans. He used Noah who was a drunkard to save humanity in a boat. He used Gideon who was hiding his wheat, a man from a poor family, to deliver the children of Israel. He used a shepherd boy, named David, to become a king.

1 Corinthians 1:27-31
27   But God hath chosen the foolish things of the world to confound the wise; and God hath chosen the weak things of the world to confound the things which are mighty;
28   And base things of the world, and things which are despised, hath God chosen, yea, and things which are not, to bring to nought things that are:
29   That no flesh should glory in his presence.
30   But of him are ye in Christ Jesus, who of God is made unto us wisdom, and righteousness, and sanctification, and redemption:
31   That, according as it is written, He that glorieth, let him glory in the Lord. (KJV)

I am so glad that He chose me. I don't know why but I'm so glad that he did. I was truly one of the foolish, weakened, debased and despised. Yet, God chose me and empowered me to live a life that brings Him glory.

I had been making a living doing carpentry and remodeling work; and in 1994, I started V.R. Thomas

Construction. I was hesitant at first. I remember telling God that I didn't have enough to start a company. I didn't have a van, and I didn't have all of the equipment or tools that a construction company uses and needs. I must have sounded like Moses when he made excuses to God why he couldn't be used to deliver the children of Israel out of Egypt. I found out that God looks past who we are and what we have. He looks beyond our past and present and sees our potential. He is the one that enables us to minister, witness, and obtain wealth in the first place.

He spoke to my spirit, so clearly, and told me to use what I had. First, I used my knowledge by passing the State of Michigan examinations and received my builder's license. Then I took my saw, hammer and drill to become a legitimate company that provided opportunities for others to be employed. God was constantly restoring my life and showing me how biblical principles work.

The two stories of the widow women in the Bible came to mind. One only had enough for her and her son to eat and soon they would die. She gave to the man of God first and was blessed many years after. I began to tithe first and found that I was never in need. The other widow woman didn't have enough oil to pay her debts, but she trusted in God. God moved miraculously and multiplied what she had so that she was able to pay her debts, and still had some to live on. She became an entrepreneur.

Now that I had steady employment, there were other areas in my life that needed restoration. My credit rating had to be taken care of. I hadn't had a legitimate job in almost 20 years. I had to pay off some debts that I had incurred over the years. I know of miraculous debt cancellation in people's lives. However, some people have to do it the old fashioned way, pay who and what they owe. My finances were being restored. God began to see that my money was multiplied. By following biblical principles of managing money and resources, I seemed to have more to work with.

I was making less money than I was when I was selling drugs, yet I was now able to hold on to more money. I had peace of mind that I never knew existed. I was making a living legitimately, without having to worry about the police arresting me. I no longer had to live with the threat of someone trying to rob and kill me. That was restoration for me. I have been blessed beyond what the original expectations that I had for myself. I no longer put limits on what God can do for me, to me or through me. He is indeed able to do exceeding, abundantly above all that I can ask or think, and I can think big.

The material blessings and restorations are nice but there are other areas of more importance that God has restored. First of all, my spiritual life and relationship with Him was restored. It is constantly growing and getting stronger. Secondly, he restored my marriage life, family life, and social standing. When God begins a good work he has completion in mind.

Philippians 1:6 states:

Being confident of this very thing, that he which hath begun a good work in you will perform {it} until the day of Jesus Christ. (KJV)

God sent a beautiful, lovely woman, that really loves Him first, into my life. I was attending an After Christ meeting ran by Pastors Rudy and Lois Ellis. These meetings were for people that were seeking to come out of lifestyles of bondage or had been delivered and were seeking strength in their relationship with God. One of the ministers that helped to facilitate the meetings was a young woman, Cynthia. Cynthia is Lois' younger sister. We met and knew each other for about a year before we started seriously dating one another. Once we started, we became engaged and married in 18 months. We had a beautiful wedding in which all of my children were a part of, except one.

Aspects where I was weak in relating to the children, Cynthia has helped in various areas tremendously. She did this without trying to take the place of their mother, yet letting them know that she was there for them. By her not pushing herself on them, it allowed their relationships to naturally evolve. As with nuclear families, there have been differences that had to be worked on and resolved. Some are still being worked out as we cope with the challenges of becoming a well-blended family. Not Perfect.

It is alarming that the divorce in the United States is around 50%. What is more devastating is the fact that it is slightly higher in Christian marriages. This was my second marriage and Cynthia's first. She married a man with five children by three different women. Cynthia is a special kind of woman to even consider entering into a marriage under those conditions. People are always asking her how she does it. God has helped the both of us tremendously.

Cynthia and I have used our experience to help minister to other families that have found themselves in this same situation. We have been teaching and speaking at seminars and conventions about coping with the challenges of blended families and developed a seminar series. My first marriage ended in divorce. Nonetheless, I was given an opportunity to experience a marriage the way God meant for it to be in the beginning.

There is a restoration that is taking place in my relationship with my children. Some people think that because their children are older that they are fine. Both estranged parent and child must be honest and confess that there have been hurts, disappointments, and to some extent, mental and emotional trauma. The pain does not disappear because estranged parents return. In some cases, you may not be openly accepted; and, if you are, forgiveness must occur in order for the relationship to be healed and restored. This is a process which takes time. Both you and the children must want it and be willing to do whatever the Bible commands to achieve it. I can see it happening in the relationships with my children. You cannot become discouraged with set backs or differences that may come up. You have to work through them and not turn your back on each other. It does get better.

God restored my health and added years to my life. Living the lifestyle that I chose, there wasn't time or concern about going to the doctor for annual checkups. The only reason for seeing a doctor was in cases of extreme emergencies. Overdoses, gunshots, stabbing, anything that was obviously a threat to my life or hindered my ability to hustle was cause for going to the doctor. Routine exams and preventive medicine were not high on my list.

I didn't start immediately but once I began going to the doctor, I went on a regular basis. I also began going to the optometrist for my eyes and the dentist. This is something that I recommend highly to everyone, seeing a physician, optometrist, and dentist for annual exams.

In 1999, I went to Dr. Shiek and Dr. in Southfield, Michigan for a routine checkup. After learning the results of my blood work, I was diagnosed with Hepatitis C. I was referred to a specialist and was informed that it was incurable, and that I would have to undergo treatment for a number of years to keep my liver enzymes at a certain level. The doctors also informed me that the disease would eventually destroy my liver. God miraculously healed me of Hepatitis C, and, today, my blood cell count and liver enzymes are within normal limits.

Healing still happens today. Healing can come in other ways as well. Most people associate healing with the miraculous. Miracles are what happen when God intervenes, moves and changes a situation that cannot be explained by natural or scientific means. Healing can be miraculous and it also can be natural or aided by the help of others such as doctors, counselors, pastors or friends. Healing is to make healthy, whole, or restore to well being from ailments and sickness.

By reading pamphlets in the doctor's office and articles in other magazines, I became aware of prostate cancer. I discovered that prostate cancer is one of the leading causes of death in Afro-American men over the age of 40. Many men, of all races, are reluctant to have their prostate checked because of the procedure used. I can honestly attest that no man is less of a man when getting tested. As a matter of fact, a wise man will get tested. It may add years to his life.

I attended a free screening that was offered, and the

results indicated that my PSA (prostate specific antigen) level was high. High levels indicate the possible presence of cancer in the prostate. It was recommended for me to see an urologist for further testing. I went to see Dr. Conrad Maitland who was on staff at Harper Hospital in Detroit. He has been my urologist ever since. After further testing, he scheduled me for a biopsy, which came back positive. I had prostate cancer. He went over the options with me and I elected to have the surgery. It was year 2000 and I was 48 years old.

I am a believer that all healing is not done by laying on of hands and that God can move on your body through the God-given gifts of doctors. Today, I am cancer free. The cancer had not spread to my lymph nodes and I still have the activity of my limb, so to speak, with nerves in tack. The wisdom of obedience brings the blessings of God. I proudly proclaim myself a cancer survivor. Nothing is too difficult for God.

God restored my social life as well as my standing in the community. I became a founding board member and Vice President of the Highland Park Business Association. A vision to make our city, which was in financial ruin, become a better place to live, work and do business. I helped to found The Highland Park Homeownership Collaborative of which I serve as the Chairman. This is a group of Non-profits that will start building new homes in our city. I also serve on the board of the Development Corporation of Wayne County. I believe, without a doubt, that what God can do in a person's life, He can also do with a city and nation. Nations and cities, like people, fall into ruin when they fall away from God and God's principles. As a pastor, I felt that a voice should be heard that would not compromise God's principles in our association. Faith Tabernacle has hosted public meetings with state, county and city officials. I have hosted and sat alongside the Police Chief and the County Sheriff. Here, me, an ex-addict, career criminal, ex-felon, and convict sitting and talking with the Sheriff and it wasn't an interrogation for some crime that I had committed. In the past, I would see the police and go in the other direction.

I was sought out and asked to sit on a Steering Committee appointed by the Governor of the State of Michigan, as a representative of the local churches. There is absolutely no one who can tell me that there is anything impossible for God to do.

God has chosen to use me and my ministry locally, nationally and internationally to spread the gospel and give hope to many people all over the world. God has chosen to use someone that was weak, debased, despised and foolish to articulate the gospel in such a powerful and mesmerizing way that many can look to Jesus Christ and realize that they too can do all things through Him.

To support the "Yes You Can" mentality, I have witnessed a young man that had a white adventurous mother, who married a black man from Kenya. The father left at an early age and the young man was raised by his mother and grandparents. He went on to finish school and obtained a Law Degree from Harvard University. He later became a State Senator in Illinois and then a United States Senator from Illinois. He is now the first African-American President of the United States, Barack Obama.

TO GOD BE THE GLORY!

Chapter 25

Yes, You Can!

After reading this book, I pray that you know without a doubt that there is hope for everybody. For those that have felt so overwhelmed and defeated by their past that it has dimmed the light of their future, I want to share some practical steps that can be followed to help in maintaining a Godly lifestyle after being delivered from any type of bondage. I go more in-depth in a seminar and workbook that I have developed for overcoming setbacks, delays and adversities entitled **"Yes I Will"**. I conduct this seminar internationally and have released it to be taught through other ministries as well.

Step 1:
Confession

The Bible instructs us to confess our faults one to another that we may be healed. A person holds so many of there past wrongs inside of them and it has the ability to eat them up from the inside. They live in torment of guilt, shame and condemnation. God desires for you to be free from these things. Christ came to save you, not to condemn you.

You must be willing to confess your sins and ask God for forgiveness.

I John 1:9
9   If we confess our sins, he is faithful and just and will forgive us our sins and purify us from all unrighteousness. (NIV)

Step 2:
Repentance

You cannot skip over this step and think that you will stay delivered. Repentance is more than feeling sorry and remorseful for your past life. It means to have a change of mind, stand in agreement with **God's Word** and *completely turn away* from your sinful activities. You are to turn toward God and stand in agreement with Him and His Word. The Prodigal Son, coming to his senses, got up and turned from the pigsty that he was living in and headed for his father's house.

It is by way of repentance that you allow God to move on your behalf to begin a restoration and healing process in your life.

2 Chronicles 7:14
14   If my people, who are called by my name, will humble themselves and pray and seek my face and turn from their wicked ways, then will I hear from heaven and will forgive their sin and will heal their land. (NIV)

Step 3:
Forgiveness

As a Christian, you have to understand that the very basis of your relationship with God is the fact that once you confess your sins, He forgives you. It is not based on how good a person you were or are now. God knows all about your past. He knows every detail that you have even carefully hidden from others. Yet, the works of Jesus Christ on the cross at Calvary has paid the price in full for your sins. Remember that God is faithful and just to forgive you.

In the same manner that God has forgiven you, you now must make a decision to forgive those that have wronged you in any way.

> Matthew 6:14-15
> 14 For if you forgive men when they sin against you, your heavenly Father will also forgive you.
> 15 But if you do not forgive men their sins, your Father will not forgive your sins. (NIV)

Forgiving another person is not something that is granted them for their benefit. It is for your benefit because it frees you up from negative emotional feelings. When you don't forgive, you allow feelings of anger, resentment, bitterness, and hate to constantly rule your emotions whenever you think of the person or see them. Forgiveness releases you from those feelings and allows for the spirit of love, peace and joy to take root in your life.

There is another area of forgiveness that is of equal importance. That is forgiving yourself just as God has forgiven you. Some people cannot except the forgiveness of God because they can't forgive themselves. While for other people they come readily to the realization that if God can forgive me, then I have to learn to forgive myself. Forgiving yourself frees you as well. It frees you from the awful feelings of not being loved, rejection, guilt, shame, fear, and inferiority.

Holding on to unforgiveness and these negative emotions can be a catalyst or trigger that can stimulate in you an urge to go back to your former lifestyle.

Step 4:
Put Off and Put On

Putting off and putting on is a replacement process. It is so important because it fills the void that is left in your life when you abandon and no longer engage in sinful thoughts, activities, behavior and lifestyle.

Here you have to put off anything that you are doing that is contrary to the Word of God. You then began to put on and do the very opposite thing that the Word of God tells you. The Scripture that best describes putting something off and replacing it with just the opposite is:

Ephesians 4:22-29

22   You were taught, with regard to your former way of life, to put off your old self, which is being corrupted by its deceitful desires;

23   to be made new in the attitude of your minds;

24   and to put on the new self, created to be like God in true righteousness and holiness.

25   Therefore each of you must put off falsehood and speak truthfully to his neighbor, for we are all members of one body.

26   "In your anger do not sin": Do not let the sun go down while you are still angry,

27   and do not give the devil a foothold.

28   He who has been stealing must steal no longer, but must work, doing something useful with his own hands, that he may have something to share with those in need.

29   Do not let any unwholesome talk come out of your mouths, but only what is helpful for building others up according to their needs, that it may benefit those who listen. (NIV)

You cannot put off things without replacing them.

There is danger in that. Take a look at the

following Scripture.

Matthew 12:43-45

43   "When an evil spirit comes out of a man, it goes through dry places seeking rest and does not find it.

44   Then it says, 'I will return to the house I left.' When it arrives, it finds the house unoccupied, swept clean and put in order.

45   Then it goes and takes with it seven other spirits more wicked
than itself, and they go in and live there. And the final condition of that man is worse than the first.

That is how it will be with this wicked generation."
(NIV)

You cannot afford to stop doing something and not replace that with something else. Your life will have a void that leaves room for that type of behavior to start again in your life with the chance of it becoming worse.

Another Scripture describing what you can put off and put on deals with the "Fruit of the Spirit."

Galatians 5:19-23
19 The acts of the sinful nature are obvious: sexual immorality, impurity and debauchery;
20 idolatry and witchcraft; hatred, discord, jealousy, fits of rage, selfish ambition, dissentions, factions
21 and envy; drunkenness, orgies, and the like. I warn you, as I did before, that those who live like this will not inherit the kingdom of God.
22 But the fruit of the Spirit is love, joy, peace, patience, kindness, goodness, faithfulness,
23 gentleness and self-control. Against such things there is no law. (NIV)

Step 5:
Develop A Continuous Prayer and Praise Life

Through prayer and praise you remain connected in fellowship with God. Your prayer life should not be where you present to God a shopping list of your wants, as if He is a spiritual Santa Claus. It should be a time of open dialogue where you talk to Him and listen for His response to your spirit. So often people have an ineffective prayer life because they ask God for guidance, support and provision, yet they do not take the time to listen to God when He wants to tell them what direction they should go in, or how He will provide the support or meet their need. Praying does not have to be a talk spoken with eloquence of speech or sprinkled with big words. Your prayers do not have to sound like you live in the Middle Ages, full of "thou, henceforth" and other words common in the King James Bible. You speak to God openly and honestly about what you are going through and how you feel. Jesus Christ promised in His Word that He would never leave you or forsake you. You are not alone. A continuous prayer life reminds you of that.

Praising God is a heart issue. It is not done according to how you feel. You praise God out of a heart and attitude of gratefulness and adoration. You praise and worship God for who He is. He is worthy of your praise. The Bible tells us that everything that has breath should praise the Lord. When you are feeling down and think that you can't praise God, just think back over your life and recall what He has delivered you from. You will find yourself being grateful and praising God.

The Book of Psalms is full of plentiful reasons to praise God. Here are just a couple of more Scripture to keep in mind.

Philippians 4:6-8
6 Do not be anxious about anything, but in everything, by prayer and petition, with thanksgiving, present your requests to God.
7 And the peace of God, which transcends all understanding, will guard your hearts and your minds in Christ Jesus.
8 Finally, brothers, whatever is true, whatever is noble, whatever is right, whatever is pure, whatever is lovely, whatever is admirable-if anything is excellent or praiseworthy-think about such things. (NIV)

Psalms 34:1
I will extol the LORD at all times; his praise will always be on my lips (NIV)

Ephesians 6:18
And pray in the Spirit on all occasions with all kinds of prayers and requests. With this in mind, be alert and always keep on praying for all the saints. (NIV)

Step 6:
Read Your Bible Daily

The Bible tells us in 2 Timothy 3:16-17 that all the Scriptures are inspired by God and are for our benefit. They were written to instruct you, guide you, correct you, and teach you. That you will be equipped to live a Godly life, a life different from the one of bondage that you came out of. Living a victorious and abundant life is a by-product of obeying the Word of God. Being obedient to the Word of God stops you from going back into your former lifestyle.

Psalms 119:11
11 I have hidden your word in my heart that I might not sin against you.
(NIV)

Step 7:
Fellowship with Other Believers

As with putting off and putting on in other areas of your life and since you are no longer associating with people from your former life, you must establish friendships and fellowship with other Christians. By staying connected with other believers, you have a support group and network of like-minded people that will encourage you in your new life of victory and deliverance.

Contrary to worldly opinions, Christians do have fun-filled and exciting lives. They are not boring people. You will find yourself living and enjoying a wholesome life with people that truly care about your well being. People that are not enticing you to live a destructive life.

Hebrews 10:23-25
23 Now we can look forward to the salvation God has promised us. There is no longer any room for doubt, and we can tell others that salvation is ours, for there is no question that he will do what he says.
24 In response to all he has done for us, let us outdo each other in being helpful and kind to each other and in doing good.
25 Let us not neglect our church meetings, as some people do, but encourage and warn each other,

especially now that the day of his coming back again
is drawing near. (TLB)

Step 8:
Submit and Commit Yourself to God

Spend time with God for He is your source of
strength and protection. By yielding your life to Him, you
distance yourself from the advances and influences of
Satan.

When a child is near his or her parents, they can be
protected better than the one that is outside of the parent's
watchful eyes. When you are closer to God, you submit to
His authority and not that of someone else. Submission is
an act of the heart and is done so willingly. It is the sign of
one that is not lifted in self or pride. When you are humble
and draw closer to God then He comes closer to you.

> James 4:6-8
> 6 But he gives more grace: Therefore he said, God
> opposes the proud but gives grace to the humble.
> 7 Submit yourselves, then, to God. Resist the devil,
> and he will flee from you.
> 8 Come near to God and he will come near to you.
> Wash your hands, you sinners, and purify your
> hearts, you double-minded. (NIV)

Step 9:
Put on The Whole Armor of God

Now that you are free from your former lifestyle
does not mean that Satan is going to stop trying to attack
your mind with sinful thoughts or entice you to return to

your old ways of doing things. Like a soldier that stays prepared for battle, you must also be prepared for the enemy that comes to kill, steal and destroy your new way of living.

Stand firm my brother and sisters in the Lord. You will be victorious.

Ephesians 6:10-18
10 Finally, be strong in the Lord and in his mighty power.
11 Put on the full armor of God so that you can take your stand against the devil's schemes.
12 For our struggle is not against flesh and blood, but against the rulers, against the authorities, against the powers of this dark world and against the spiritual forces of evil in the heavenly realms.
 13 Therefore put on the full armor of God, so that when the day of evil comes, you may be able to stand your ground, and after you have done everything, to stand.
14 Stand firm then, with the belt of truth buckled around your waist, with the breastplate of righteousness in place,
15 and with your feet fitted with the readiness that comes from the gospel of peace.
16 In addition to all this, take up the shield of faith, with which you can extinguish all the flaming arrows of the evil one.
17 Take the helmet of salvation and the sword of the Spirit, which is the word of God. (NIV)

Step 10:
Know Your New Identity in Jesus Christ

To say that you are now a Christian is good.

However, there are specific descriptions that the Word of God says that you are, now that you are a believer. In Philippians 4:8, the Bible tells us to think on the good, honest, just, and true things. Well, you can think on these Scriptures that tell who you are and confess them positively.

You may want to declare daily the... "I AM'S...."

I AM	A child of God	Roman 8:14-16
I AM	A heir and joint-heir with Christ Roman 8:17	
I AM	A member of Christ's body 1 Cor. 12:27	Eph. 5:30
I AM	A branch of Christ who is the true vine John 15:1;5	
I AM	Loved by Christ	John 15:9
I AM	Friend of Christ	John 15:15
I AM	Chosen and appointed by Christ to bear his fruit John 15:16	
I AM	Righteous and holy	Eph. 4:24
I AM	Hidden in God with Christ Col. 3:3	
I AM	Part of a chosen race, a royal priesthood, a holy nation for God's Possession to proclaim His excellence and glory (1 Pet.2:9-10)	